WALKING BOOK

DR. MARCHETTI'S

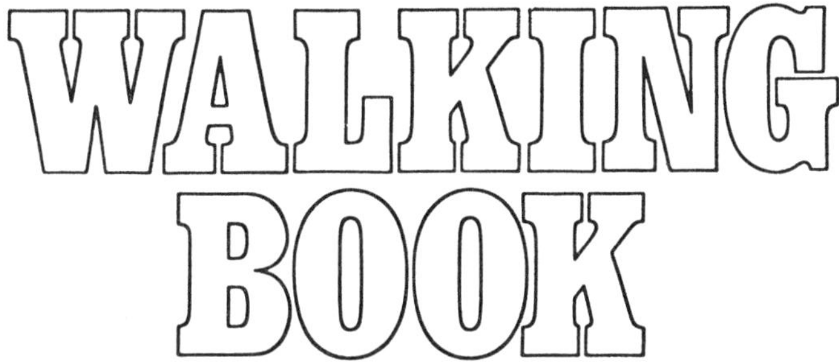

A Doctor's Guide to a Longer, Healthier Life Through a Daily Program of Walking Exercises

Albert Marchetti, M.D.

SD

STEIN AND DAY/*Publishers*/New York

First published in 1980

Designed by Louis Ditizio
Printed in the United States of America
Stein and Day/*Publishers*/Scarborough House
Briarcliff Manor, N.Y. 10510

Library of Congress Cataloging in Publication Data
Marchetti, Albert.
Dr. Marchetti's walking book.

1. Walking. 2. Exercise. I. Title. II. Title:
Walking book.
RA781.M382 613.7'1 78-66258
ISBN 0-8128-2611-6

Also by Albert Marchetti, M. D.
Common Cures for Common Ailments

To the turtles,
for the race is not always to the swiftest.

Special Acknowledgment

To Elizabeth Spedale, R.P.T., for her assistance and encouragement

Contents

Introduction

A daily program of exercise is an essential part of any normal, healthy life. A daily program of exercise is essential to the prevention of disease. But what exercise is the safest and best? What exercise has proven conditioning benefit yet can be enjoyed any time, anywhere by anyone, regardless of age, sex, or fitness? What exercise contributes most to longevity? What exercise is best? What exercise can I as a doctor recommend with confidence to everyone?

Without hesitation it would be the aerobic walking program outlined in this book. Aerobic walking is the one best means of eliminating sickness and suffering from your life while extending your life expectancy.

Two million years ago when man first stood erect, he left the realm of the four-legged animals, the runners, and became earth's supreme walker. Today, as then, walking still holds the key to man's future, his health, and life.

Walking is the most efficient exercise for man. The human body literally evolved for it.

Walking strengthens muscles and bones.

Walking improves heart and lung reserves.

Walking reduces the overall risk of heart attack and prevents sudden death from heart attacks.

Walking prevents obesity.

Walking reduces stress as effectively as tranquillizers.

Walking aids digestion.

Walking prevents or reverses adult-onset diabetes.

Walking improves the quality of life.

Walking improves man's lifespan.

Since walking is a true aerobic exercise, it is just as effective in promoting fitness as running, jogging, swimming, or cycling. In fact, when performed properly, it is even better than these other forms of exercise because it is safer.

This book provides a daily walking plan that requires only 25 minutes of your time and no special equipment or training. My walking program is for everyone, but holds the greatest promise for non-exercisers, young and old.

Few adults are true walkers. Most simply saunter or stroll from place to place. To derive the desired benefits of good health and long life, walking must be done properly. And the most controlled method is to pulse monitor your activity. All of the instructions for pulse monitoring are in the book, along with charts that depict proper exercising heart rates for all ages. There are instructions for the correct method of taking the pulse, and special conditions for cardiac patients and other physically impaired people are outlined. Weekly charts are provided so that the reader can keep track of his progress.

Unlike other exercises or sports, walking has absolutely no time limitations. Any time is well spent. If you have fifteen minutes you can walk a mile.

In addition to finding in this book all the information you will need to set up your own personal walking program, you will find a chapter devoted to walking exercises. These are a series of calisthenic exercises that are performed while walking to improve, strengthen, and slim specific parts of the body, including the face.

The format of instruction for your walking program is straightforward. Initially, in the BEFORE section, you will learn about the hazards to your health that inactivity promotes—the illnesses that befall us all because of our "civilized" lifestyles and our lazy ways. You will be helped to focus on your potential or pre-existing medical problems and examine the different methods that might alleviate them. You will discover that not all exercises are created equally—walking is by far the best.

Next, in the DURING section, you will find out how to walk aerobically—how fast, how far, and how frequently you must work out in order to achieve excellent health, and what exercise methods are used most successfully by doctors around the world. You will also learn how to follow your progress and monitor the beneficial changes that occur in your body.

Finally, in the BEYOND segment, alternatives to our lazy lifestyles are suggested along with a discussion on how to change our surroundings to better our health. With a knowledge of what can be done, you will be able to implement the necessary corrections and avoid many of the medical maladies that society creates for us.

BEFORE

You are undoubtedly aware of the problem. . . . It confronts you every time you look in a mirror. You know you should be getting more exercise, and more often, if only . . .

Before we can solve any problem, we need to understand exactly why it exists. Then we have to find the personal motivation to implement a solution. These are the absolute requirements of any self-help program.

CHAPTER I

The Problem

I'm sure you have watched such notables as Dr. Kildare, Ben Casey, and Marcus Welby perform medical miracles on television. Perhaps you have even had a fantasy or two of assisting these good doctors as they stamped out disease and saved lives. (Pass the scalpel: Watch out, doctor, that patient is going to be trouble!) Well, now I'm going to give you a chance—it's your turn to play doctor, with a little medical assistance from me.

To start, let's examine two case histories. I'll describe the illnesses for you and provide the medical data. Then (after the commercial, of course) you should attempt to determine a diagnosis and think out the appropriate treatment. Ready? Here we go . . .

Case History No. 1.

June, a divorcee, is a hard-working secretary caught up in the daily grind of making a living and raising a family. She would spend 8-10 hours a day, six days a week, on the job, then she would go home at night and take care of her two children. Overweight, smoking two packs of cigarettes a day, and drinking a little too much, she was literally a walking time bomb. First came the nervous breakdown, which was treated with three tranquilizers a day, then came the ulcer that required surgery. After an extended hospital stay following her operation, she has been discharged and placed under your care.

Case History No. 2.

Henry is a slim, handsome 44-year-old C.P.A. who lives a life of moderation, neither eating nor drinking to excess. He works reasonable hours, five days a week, and on weekends finds time to relax. Recognizing the need to stay in shape, he would occasionally jog or play handball—he thought he was fit. Everyone was surprised when Henry suffered a heart attack one Sunday morning on the handball court.

Now, what diagnosis would you make in each case? You would order June to cut down on her smoking and drinking, of course, and you would advise her not to work so hard. Perhaps you'd suggest a diet.

Turning to Henry's case, you may be a bit baffled. A heart attack out of the blue? Well, let's order some tests. Perhaps an EKG—you've heard of this one and seen TV patients hooked up to this incredible-looking machine with its needles and graph paper. But why did this "healthy" man have a heart attack in the first place? That may seem a medical mystery to you.

Actually, Henry was in trouble before he ever stepped out on the handball court. In fact, he and June shared the same basic medical debility. Surprised? Yes, these two seemingly dissimilar individuals both belong in the same disastrous file. They both had one critical factor in common, although in Henry's case it was not conspicuous—neither exercised on a daily basis. They both were deconditioned, basically unhealthy, and likely to succumb to the first serious stress that came along. Hopefully, their example will enlighten you.

If *you* don't exercise regularly, and you think you're in good shape, forget it—you're sadly mistaken. I don't care how trim you look or what type of work you do; without a *daily* exercise program, it is impossible for you to stay fit. Let me tell you why.

Human beings are nothing more than large animals. The only thing that separates us from all the other creatures on earth is the size of our brain and our capacity to learn and reason. But like all other animals, we must remain physically active to stay healthy. Otherwise, like the captive animals in a zoo, we will suffer through many illnesses and die young.

During our childhood, before we consciously avoided physical activity, we were on the go constantly. We burned up energy like rockets blazing into outer space, partly due to our ceaseless activity, partly due to the furious metabolism that is a natural part of the growth process. We could eat anything we wanted and never needed an exercise program. In fact, it has frequently been stated that the best conditioned athlete, pound for pound, is the average nine-year-old child. Just watch one in action for a few minutes and you will immediately know what I mean.

As we get older, however, our bodies undergo disastrous changes that are detrimental to our well-being. Increasingly less active because of our lazy, civilized lifestyles, we slow down and our metabolic rate slows down with us. The slower we get, the slower it gets until . . .

No wonder I hear patients and friends, people who come from all walks of life, mournfully mumble the same complaints: "I just can't eat as much as I used to. I always feel so tired, I have no energy. I guess I'm getting older." Although they don't want to accept it, in most cases they are absolutely correct in their appraisals. Of course they can't eat as much; their metabolism is half what it was during their childhood. Naturally they don't have much energy, their lifestyles don't demand it. And since they do nothing about it, they *are* getting older, and faster than they think.

To me, their complaints are symptoms. I have seen or heard them time and time again. Normally, these symptoms are but the result of a lack of exercise, pure and simple. But that's only half the problem. They are also the initial signs of heart disease, high blood pressure, obesity, diabetes, and other diseases related to inactivity. And—I must tell you this right now—just about every disease imaginable is in some way related to inactivity. Even some forms of cancer.

I'm sure you have been aware of many of these things for some time, whether you sought out medical information or not. After all, for years doctors have been pointing out the destructive effect of inactivity on good health and well-being.

For these reasons, I want you to read this book. Then, I want you to apply my *Ten Walking Rules* to your life, today, tomorrow, and forever. I want you to be happy and healthy. The road to those life goals lies right at your feet. Literally! Let me tell you why.

Like most adults, I have been fighting a battle with my body. By the time I was 26 and graduated from medical school, I was already out of control. The natural fitness of my youth was gradually fading. I was slowly becoming a soft American, sedentary and inactive. Luckily for me, however, through four years of medical education I had begun to appreciate my body's absolute need for exercise. But my true awakening was still to come.

In 1973, I entered a postgraduate program of study at Tampa General Hospital in Florida. There, as part of my training, I performed over 200 autopsies, and witnessed another 800. I studied, firsthand, the disastrous effects inactivity had on the human body and what I learned staggered me.

From flabby hearts with thickened, clogged blood vessels to blackened lungs that could not even expand, I saw it all. Intestines surrounded with fat. Skeletal muscles, even in the young, too weak and too soft for any laborious task. Varicose veins, diabetes, fragile bones, arthritis; the list is endless. Sadly, pitifully, I saw the bodies of people who had died too young, far short of their normal life expectancy. And the cause of it all . . . inactivity.

That's when it hit me. Having seen the deadly effect inactivity has on the entire body, I decided right then and there I wanted none of it. That's when I became determined to apply the medical knowledge I had gained through years of study to the betterment of my own life. Wisely, I made my change for the better and literally saved my life. Now, I want to save yours. The key is exercise.

I understand exercise is hard to get, especially in our highly technical and automated society. For convenience, possibly from force of habit, we drive cars, ride buses, trains, cabs, and subways. Due to the nature of our work, we sit at our desks eight hours a day, five days a week, hardly moving a muscle. Finally, exhausted from minimal exertion, we go home and read or watch television. Night after night, the pattern repeats itself, carrying right into the weekend. We're so tired that *this* weekend we'll just relax. *Next* weekend we'll get some exercise. But somehow that "next weekend" never seems to arrive. So we eat. We sleep. Then we get up and ride in our cars back to work, starting the routine all over again.

But this simply can't go on. If it does, we will all experience the horrible consequences. We must do something more. We all must exercise every day. And I have developed the program to make it possible for anyone, more especially, for you, to exercise.

But why my program? What can be so special about it? What will my *Ten Walking Rules* do for you once you've finished this book?

Well, to start, I have eliminated the greatest pitfalls to successful exercising—drudgery, the gasping for air, the extreme exhaustion, and the feelings of internal revolt. I'll show you how to regulate the intensity of your exercise so you will never again feel uncomfortable or overexert yourself while you work out. In fact, you will know when to slow down! (Chapter 4)

As you progress through the first weeks of my program, you will immediately notice the benefits to your health. Easy tests will allow you to measure your progress, thus providing constant reinforcement and objective evidence of improvement. You will be encouraged by *results* to keep going until you have reached your ultimate objective—excellent physical fitness and the best of health.

Since I have selected walking, the most sensible exercise of all, you will be easily able to enter my program, regardless of your present age or physical condition. And, because the entire routine is only 12 minutes each day (plus a short warming-up and cooling-off period) you can never again complain: "I have no time."

The simplicity of my program cannot be overemphasized. By following the instructions, step by step, all the guesswork is taken out of exercise. You will be able to structure a routine that is tailored specifically to you. All the charts, graphs, guidelines, and timetables you will ever need are here in this book. I even help schedule an exercise program into your day, so it won't be forgotten or put off until tomorrow. Indeed, that is one of the major objectives of my *Ten Walking Rules.* (Chapter 10)

My exercise program is based on crucial information from a myriad of sources, but it won't do you a bit of good *until you* respond. Get into the program, give it a try. I know you won't regret it. In fact, I am sure you will enjoy every minute of it, right from the start. You will feel healthier and happier—and that's only the beginning.

Let's go.

CHAPTER 2

What Exercises Are Best?

Whenever a doctor recommends exercise, he must be very specific because there are so many variables. Certainly, your age, health, and physical condition must figure into the decision, so an exercise most suited to your individual needs can be chosen. In addition, the intensity, duration, and frequency of that exercise must be established in order to insure the proper conditioning effects. With so many variables, the decision would seem rather complicated, right? Wrong!

Thanks to medical research, the perplexing questions—how much, how long, and how often—have all been answered, even for special cases, such as cardiac and pulmonary patients. Yet, one question still persists in the minds of even the most learned physicians: Of all possible exercises, which one is actually the best? Surely, if my colleagues have trouble deciding on an individual basis, how in the world can I generalize?

For instance, should I recommend one of the isometric exercises? Remember them? By tensing one set of muscles against another, or against an immovable object such as a door jamb, supposedly you were able to achieve excellent physical fitness in just 60 seconds a day. Just 60 seconds! With a pitch like that, it's no wonder that these exercises gained immediate popularity when they were first introduced several years ago. However, when people began to realize that they just didn't work, their initial appeal gradually faded and they eventually fell into disfavor.

Sure, isometric exercises can increase overall muscular size and shape, but not in 60 seconds a day as was first promised. In this short period of time, only a few muscle groups could be exercised, perhaps those in the arms, while the rest of the body was neglected. Besides, isometrics do absolutely nothing to strengthen your heart and lungs (a major consideration in useful exercise) and their total effect on general fitness and conditioning is low. Consequently, there's no way I could recommend them as a primary exercise for you; they are truly insufficient for your daily exercise requirements.

Maybe I should prescribe an isotonic exercise, like weight lifting, calisthenics, or yoga.

Well, here again you'll run into problems if that is all that you do. You see, isotonics are very similar to isometrics. Both strengthen and enlarge skeletal muscles through repeated or sustained contractions, but neither will increase endurance or cardiovascular reserves nor will they help to prevent illness. This is not to say that isotonics are useless, however; that statement would be terribly misleading. When used intelligently, they can add size, shape, and firmness to your body. In fact, I do them myself, the familiar push-ups and sit-ups we all know. But I certainly don't count on them for overall fitness. They simply can't do the job.

If you doubt my word about isometrics or isotonics, try a few yourself. Do 20 sit-ups, or stand in a door jamb and push against the sides for ten seconds. Has your heart rate increased significantly? Are you breathing heavily? Probably not unless you are incredibly out of shape. And that's my point. While your stomach and arm muscles might be exercised, your heart and lungs, the organs that really count, haven't been worked on at all. You truly need something more if your want to achieve total fitness, and the answer is aerobic exercise.

By their very nature, aerobic exercises are those that demand oxygen. In fact, the word "aerobic" literally means "oxygen" or "air." Whenever you perform any physical task, your body must expend energy. In this respect, you are no different than any fuel-burning, internal combustion engine. Only the fuel you burn is not gasoline or kerosene or wood; it is the food you eat. As this food combines with oxygen, heat and energy are released so work can be done.

Unlike isometrics and isotonics, aerobic exercises are unique in that they significantly increase the body's demand for energy and, in so doing, they also increase the body's need for oxygen. The harder you work, the more oxygen you will need. Consequently, the lungs must work harder to supply the precious gas, and the heart must beat faster to deliver it to the exercising muscles. Eventually, if you exercise at the proper pace, a steady state is created and an equilibrium between oxygen supply and demand is established. Once you reach this point, you could exercise almost indefinitely because you have coordinated your body functions at a higher level of energy expenditure.

But aerobic exercises do more than just burn up oxygen. By forcing the lungs to work harder, they enhance the elasticity of the lung tissue and increase the strength of the muscles that expand and contract the chest, thus enabling more oxygen to be processed with greater efficiency. Indeed, a conditioned man can move two to three times as much oxygen through his lungs than a man who is out of shape.

Aerobic exercises also strengthen the heart by causing it to beat at an accelerated rate with more forceful contractions. Just as your stomach muscles firm up with the repeated contractions that are required to perform sit-ups, and your arm muscles strengthen from push-ups, so too does your heart grow stronger and more fit through the increased number of forceful contractions that result from exercising aerobically.

Aerobic exercises increase the number and size of blood vessels throughout the body—a most incredible feat. As the body cries out for more oxygen, the heart and lungs respond accordingly. So do the millions of blood vessels that are needed to carry the oxygen. They widen and lengthen, multiply and branch, until they saturate every conceivable cubic centimeter of your body's tissue—your muscles, your heart, your lungs, your brain, your internal organs, your skin, everywhere.

Aerobic exercises also expand the blood volume, thus increasing its capacity to carry oxygen.

They change fat to lean as they burn up calories and stimulate the metabolism. And they also lower the blood pressure and decrease the resting heart rate.

Needless to say, I am clearly in favor of aerobic exercise, and I am not alone. Everyone who understands the principles of physical conditioning and true overall fitness agrees: aerobics are best. And doctors all around the world have collectively come to the conclusion that aerobic exercise does more to preserve good health and prolong life than any other form of physical activity.

But the good news about aerobics is hardly revolutionary. In fact, you may have already been urged to incorporate these exercises into your daily lives. Only instead of aerobics, you were told about jogging or running, cycling or jumping rope. At the time, it probably all sounded as exciting as dry toast. Now, all of the exercises I named above certainly do fall into the aerobic category. Each is a steady and continuous activity that significantly increases the heart and respiratory rates and holds them at an elevated level for a prolonged period of time. But you were hoping that I would come up with something new and exciting, something you had never heard of before.

Actually, the problem isn't with you—it's with what you've been told or have read about them. Individually, these exercises have either been given a dull presentation, seemed faddish, or appeared expensive. Worse yet, they all come on a bit strenuous and frequently intimidate would-be exercisers, discouraging rather than encouraging their participation in a much-needed exercise program. You may have dismissed this whole group of exercises in disgust.

But if you have, you've made a critical mistake. Because of all the possible exercises you could choose to perform, aerobics are the best. And there's one in particular that stands out above all the rest. It is the easiest, the safest, the most practical, and the most applicable. It is, at last, the aerobic exercise for you.

Let's take a little walk. . . .

CHAPTER 3

Walking: The Best Exercise of All

Personally, I think that the ultimate exercise should be enjoyable and still provide the aerobic benefits of good health and excellent physical conditioning. In addition, it should have a broad appeal and be something everyone can do regardless of their sex, age, wealth, or pre-existing physical condition. And for convenience, it must be an "anywhere, anytime" exercise that can be performed during work or play, in a suit or a dress or an exercise outfit. I know it sounds like a tall order, but such an exercise does exist.

What I'm thinking of is the most natural form of physical activity we can get. It was the first lasting exercise most of us performed during our early childhood and will probably be the last one we will ever do. Some people say it's as natural to us as breathing. Because it's so simple and at times even effortless, many people don't even think of it as exercise. But believe me, it's terrific, and its time has come. The best exercise of all is *walking.*

How can this be, you might wonder? Can walking be better than cycling or tennis or swimming? Surely, it can't compare to running, the physical phenomenon that has received so much attention in the last few years. Walking is just too easy!

Well, I'd be the last person to tell you that the other aerobic exercises are no good. Each has its own value and is absolutely beneficial in terms of providing mental and physical well-being. But walking is the best as far as I'm concerned, and the best on the basis of all considerations. Here's why.

As I pointed out in Chapter 2, aerobic exercises are the true conditioning exercises—they do the most for your heart and lungs. By stimulating new blood vessel growth and increasing the oxygenation of all the tissues of the body, they revitalize and rejuvenate. By building the body's energy reserves, they increase endurance and physical performance. All of the aerobic exercises, including walking, achieve the same end results, so they are all equal in their healthful benefits. This is a fact, not merely an opinion.

Through the observations and experiments that Dr. Kenneth Cooper conducted in the sixties, he demonstrated absolutely the equality of similar levels of aerobic activity. He proved that walkers were as fit as runners, swimmers, and cyclists. If each activity was performed to the limits he prescribed, they all generated a good-to-excellent physical state. Walking was no exception. In fact, it was ranked up there with much more strenuous and demanding exercises such as jogging and running. Again, fact, not opinion.

On the strength of this information, I became fascinated with the whole idea of walking as an exercise. After all, if it conditioned the body as thoroughly as running, swimming, and cycling (and Cooper proved that it did), it had to be highly beneficial and yet remarkably easy. I began thinking about it more and more.

Now I'm not a novice when it comes to physical fitness. At the time of my rude awakening during my postdoctoral training in pathology, I became somewhat obsessed with exercise. Although I only run intermittently, I did turn out seven minute miles with the best of them. Three miles in 20 minutes is now my personal standard. I also swim—20, 30, sometimes 40 laps—for upper body exercise. And racquetball is another of my favorites. But not everyone can swim or play racquetball, and many people dislike running. What then should they do? Must they resign themselves to a life of inactivity with all of its medical hazards and pitfalls? Of course not! Obviously there must be an acceptable alternative. And the alternative is walking.

To test my theory, I started a walking program of my own. Whenever I was traveling, unable to swim or run, I would walk. Through the big city streets I literally walked for hours—it was great. Along thoroughfares, across fields and parks, down small country roads; it didn't matter. Wherever I was, each walk was completely enjoyable and absolutely beneficial in terms of fulfilling my need and desire to exercise.

The more I walked, the more I realized the rewards. Although I am an occasional runner, walking further tightened my legs and buttocks. Much to my amazement, it also relieved the back discomfort that so often annoyed me and which frequently becomes worse when I run. Walking was wonderful.

I began to research the concept of walking as a total exercise and many positive points came to my attention. Compared to all other sports or physical activities, walking has the fewest number of complications or risks; in fact, it has virtually none at all. Swimmers, for example, can suffer from eye problems associated with wearing goggles or ear maladies that include everything from superficial infections to painful boney growths, osteomas, in the external ear canal. Tennis players can sustain eye injuries from being hit in the face by a racquet or a ball. And who hasn't heard of tennis elbow—a painful inflammation of the elbow joint that so frequently plagues avid players?

Worse yet are the broken bones that result from diving accidents and from rough contact sports like football and rugby, the arm fractures from wrestling, and the broken ankles from skiing: injuries that are all too common, injuries that can even kill.

Medical literature contains literally thousands and thousands of articles about all kinds of injuries related to just about every sport imaginable. The titles alone are devastating: "Transverse Fractures of the Humerus in the Shotputter," "Hand Paresthesis after Racquetball," "Thumb Neuroma: a Hazard of the Ten Pin Bowler," "Frisbee Finger," "Golfers' Fractures of the Ribs"—unbelievable! Interestingly, there was no mention of any injuries associated with walking. After a thorough search of world literature, I could find no articles on the hazards of walking, not one!

But upon further investigation, I began to uncover a wealth of information about the risks of running. Sure, it's one of the best conditioning exercises of all. But running definitely has major drawbacks, and you should know about them.

To begin, even jogging, much less out-and-out running, contributes to more heart attacks and cardiac deaths than all other exercises combined. It is so dangerous, in fact, that doctors are obliged to advise their patients over age 35 to be extremely careful when starting any kind of jogging program. Otherwise, a healthy person might go out and commit involuntary suicide by jogging only a couple of laps, just a few times around the block.

Dr. Leon Resnekov in his section of *Sports Medicine: Pathology* entitled "Jogging and Coronary Artery Disease" writes, "To obtain objective evidence of the subject's ability to tolerate an exercise program, a preliminary treadmill test with constant EKG (electrocardiogram) monitoring and full resuscitative equipment at hand should always be performed before recommending unsupervised jogging sessions." He goes on to describe three catastrophic cases to strengthen his point: one man suffered a massive heart attack while jogging, another unscreened subject went into shock when his heart stopped, and a third fell to the floor in cardiac arrest during the preliminary EKG testing session. Obviously, jogging can be a dangerous business.

Even if the novice jogger or runner survives a heart attack, his physical being from that point on is greatly impaired. Functioning with less heart muscle, having a decreased cardiac reserve, and possibly an erratic heart beat, he or she could be in constant peril. And these are but a few of the problems facing joggers and runners. There are many other injuries, from the annoying to the debilitating, waiting out there for you after you've laced up those brand new, expensive track shoes and prepared yourself to run.

On the other hand, the novice walker has nothing to fear. One, two, even three miles are no problem, not even on the first day. Sure, you might develop a blister or two, but compared to a myocardial infarction, commonly known as a heart attack, that's a small price to pay. And absolutely insignificant, I might add, when compared to the fabulous health benefits that walking bestows on its participants.

My research and initial experiences only enhance the theory: if you want to exercise *safely*—walk! If you want to exercise *effectively*—walk! And, as I will explain in later chapters, if you want an exercise program you can follow for the rest of your life—walk!

So don't be surprised if I tell you to put down this book and immediately apply the walking principles I've discussed. Think of it—with no other training, no lessons, no special equipment, and no mental brainwashing, you can do it right away. And do it successfully.

Now, isn't that the way it should be?

CHAPTER 4

How Much Is Enough

Now that you know what exercise is best for you, the next question that arises is: how much is enough? How long and how far must you walk each day in order to regain your fitness and stay in the best of health?

This is not a new question, nor is it unique to you. For years, all exercisers were baffled by the subject of exercise duration and had to approach the problem haphazardly because there were no guidelines. Some would exercise as long as they felt energetic, quitting at the first sign of fatigue. Others would push themselves to the point of exhaustion, often requiring several days to recuperate. But this guesswork approach was too unpredictable, too unreliable to produce consistently good results. A concrete program with definite goals and limits seemed imperative.

Then came Dr. Kenneth Cooper. Through his observations

and studies in exercise physiology, he answered the questions of exercise duration and produced the sorely needed guidelines for graded physical exertion, not only for runners, swimmers, and joggers, but for most other exercisers as well, including walkers.

According to his original work, which was based on the study of several thousand mostly unfit and somewhat unhealthy participants, the key to successful physical conditioning and the wonderful health benefits it bestows resided in the exercising heart rate—the number of times your heart beats each minute you are physically active. Using very sophisticated medical equipment, he followed the progress of thousands of ordinary people who needed exercise, people like you and me, and found that full aerobic benefit was realized only if the exercisers raised their heart rates to 150 beats per minute and sustained that rate for 12 consecutive minutes. It didn't matter how far they ran or swam. It didn't matter how fast or slow they had to go. *As long as they elevated their heart rate to the prescribed level and maintained that level for twelve consecutive minutes, tiptop fitness would result.*

Cooper also found that exercising only once or twice a week was too infrequent. Although each workout was beneficial, no significant improvement to health and fitness was realized. Instead, each participant simply stayed at his or her original level of stamina, neither getting better nor worse.

However, when the exercise was performed four or five times each week, rather than one or two, a marked improvement in physical conditioning resulted and all the fabulous aerobic effects began to develop in the exercisers. Slowly but surely, as the benefits added up, they became manifest in the form of higher scores on the exercise testing equipment and obvious improvements in general health and vitality. Some pre-existing diseases were even reversed.

Ultimately, Cooper reduced his program to a system of points, 30 points being needed each week to promote excellent health and physical conditioning. To this day his approach is valid, and utilizing his revised principles, I can design a custom program for you. Here's how.

Each of us has a maximum heart rate which is dependent on our age. The younger we are, the faster our maximum rate, the older, the slower. For example, the maximum heart rate for an individual 20 years of age or younger is about 200 beats per minute. Yet, an individual 60 years of age or older has a maximum rate of only 150 beats per minute. If you are between the ages of 20 and 60, your maximum rate will fall somewhere between 200 and 150.

Now, a maximum heart rate is just that. It is maximum output, top speed—the fastest your heart can beat under normal circumstances. It is the speed your heart will achieve when you exercise too vigorously. But racing your heart at this speed is like driving your car as fast as it will go. With the accelerator to the floor, sooner or later something's got to give. Your heart is no different. Running it at top speed is equally risky, since cardiac overload could quickly lead to heart failure or some other disastrous consequence.

With this in mind, you can easily see that uncontrolled exercise is very dangerous. Running around the block just a few times or swimming only a couple of laps can raise your heart rate to the critical maximum level, especially if you are out of shape. To prevent this overexertion and block the potentially dangerous side effects, an individually-tailored, well-controlled program is absolutely necessary.

As a case in point, consider this example of one of my medical associates.

A short while ago, I was speaking with a friend, Ed, who is a medical technologist at Tampa General Hospital. During our conversation, Ed told me that he had been using specific laboratory blood tests to follow his heart chemistry while on a jogging binge, and much to his amazement he had noted the presence of CPK2 and a flipped LDH pattern. What this means is that he had gotten the results that usually indicate a heart attack. Needless to say, Ed was worried; he's only 26 years old!

When I questioned him about the intensity of his exercise, he looked perplexed. "What do you mean, intensity? I just get out there and run as hard as I can for a mile. Isn't that what you're supposed to do?"

Well, that's what most people do, but that's not what you're supposed to do by any means. In fact, that was probably Ed's whole problem. Not only had he picked a grueling exercise, he also went about it too aggressively. As I explained to him then, not knowing how to monitor his pulse as he exercised, he probably pushed his heart to extremes, far beyond the limits of safety. Instead of strengthening his heart, he was actually breaking down heart muscle fibers and releasing the heart enzymes he had picked up in his lab tests. While he didn't have a heart attack, he did abuse his heart. Certainly, he had done more harm than good.

Now you must realize that Ed's situation is common. Most people, especially enthusiastic new exercisers determined to shape up quickly, overexert themselves each time they work out. By the time they finish their daily routine, they wind up totally exhausted and battered. If they were exercising properly, this would never happen; in fact, they would scarcely get out of breath. Using the simple pulse-monitored method, based on maximum heart rates, all exercisers will get results safely.

Now, perhaps, you can understand why I introduced the subject of heart rates in the first place. Each maximum heart rate, which is primarily dependent on age, is listed for you in Table A. A quick examination of the list will identify your maximum rate and provide you with the basis for your personal exercise program. It is the most important information you can have in determining your capacity to exercise. It is your supreme guideline because it is the number that is used in the exercise formula:

E H R = 75% M H R
*E*xercise *H*eart *R*ate = 75% *M*aximum *H*eart *R*ate

That's right, by maintaining a heart rate which is 75 percent of your maximum rate, you will train at the proper pace, realizing all of the aerobic benefits, without the risk of overdoing it. You will help your heart, not hurt it as Ed did. You will exercise moderately and safely according to the most critical factor, your age.

For example, if you are 30 years old, your maximum heart rate is 190 beats per minute (Table A, column 1) and your proper exercise heart rate is 75 percent of 190, or 143 beats per minute (Table A, column 3). But, if you are 60 years old, your exercise heart rate should not even approach 143 beats per minute. Rather, you should maintain a rate of only 120 beats per minute, which is 75 percent of your maximum 160.

This precise method of exercising, maintaining 75 percent of your maximum heart rate, has been shown to work extremely well, time and time again, in test after test. It is the method prescribed by cardiologists, exercise physiologists, and physical therapists around the world. It is the method you will use in my walking program.

Initially, when you enter the program, walking at a moderate pace will push your heart rate to the proper aerobic target zone,

75 percent of your maximum rate. However, the more you walk, the faster you will have to go, the harder you will have to push yourself in order to maintain your 75 percent requirement. By taking your pulse with techniques I will soon discuss, you will know exactly how you are doing; speeding up or slowing down as your pulse dictates to sustain the 75 percent level. In time, you will be walking as fast as some people jog, but, once you have reached this point, you will be able to keep up your pace effortlessly because you will have brought yourself successfully

TABLE A

Age	Maximum Heart Rate	85% Athletic Training Rate	75% Regular Training Rate	70% Cardiac Training Rate	70% Low Pulse Training Rate
20	200	170	150	140	140
22	198	168	148	138	138
24	196	167	147	137	137
26	194	165	145	135	135
28	192	163	144	134	134
30	190	162	143	133	133
32	189	161	142	132	132
34	187	159	140	130	130
36	186	158	139	130	130
38	184	156	138	129	129
40	182	155	137	127	127
45	179	152	134	125	125
50	175	149	131	122	122
55	171	145	128	120	120
60	160	136	120	112	112
65+	150	128	113	105	105

through weeks of progressive training. And that's the beauty of my program. It's simple, it's progressive, it's safe, and it really works.

I do have two cautions, however. If you have a history of heart disease—a previous heart attack or any other cardiac abnormality—exercising at 75 percent maximum might be too much for you. Instead, I recommend that you raise your heart rate to only 70 percent of its maximum output. You can follow the guidelines in Table A, column 4, and the advice in Chapter 16. Please heed this caution, for it would truly be unfortunate to sustain further damage to your heart through overexertion, especially when you have sought exercise to improve your cardiac condition. It is also a good idea for you to get medical clearance from your personal physician before you undertake my program or any other, for that matter. Although doctors around the world are now advising their cardiac patients to exercise at the 70% maximum level, your own physician should always be informed of your intentions to start an exercise program. Since walking is the safest of all exercises, I'm sure he will approve, but he might have additional instructions for you.

The second caution goes out to individuals who have very low *resting* pulses. The average is approximately 78 beats per minute; however, some people have pulses as low as 50-60 beats per minute at rest. If you are one of these people, or if you have a resting pulse that is 15 beats per minute below the average, it would be excessive for you to exercise at the 75 percent standard, since that level is set for people with higher resting pulses. For you, exercising at 70 percent maximum is better. Simply refer to Table A, column 5, for your correct exercising pulse. And don't feel slighted. You will be getting the same benefit as someone who must exercise at the 75 percent level.

Now that you know about correct exercising pulse rates, I am sure you must wonder how much time you must spend walking each day. Is it the 12 minutes that Cooper suggested or some longer period of time, maybe an hour or more? Well, walking for an hour would certainly improve health and fitness but it would also cut deeply into constructive working time and few people would accept this. Luckily, it is unnecessary. Most experts agree with Cooper and accept a 12-minute period of nonstop activity as sufficient. But remember, that's 12 consecutive minutes at the proper exercising pulse. And when walking, it might actually take 5-10 minutes just to reach this pulse level. Therefore, it becomes obvious that walking from start to finish for only 12 nonstop minutes is simply not enough. You must allow yourself at least eight minutes to warm up (Chapter 6); eight short minutes to reach your exercising pulse. Then clock off the all-important 12 consecutive minutes. That's 20 minutes in all. Twenty minutes to good health. Twenty minutes to prevent illness. Twenty minutes to improve your life. If you walk more than this, fine. But less than this is absolutely inadequate. And don't think you can walk 40 minutes today, then skip tomorrow. That won't work either. You must stick with the program exactly as I have developed it if you want results.

Here's one other point you might consider. While most of you will have no trouble, there will be a few who will find it impossible to reach the 75 percent maximum pulse rate no matter how fast they walk. If you are one of these people, it means that you are already in relatively good condition, and your heart is strong enough to meet moderate exercise challenges like brisk walking without much difficulty. For you, the walking program requires one modification. Once you have recorded the highest pulse you can achieve by walking at a *very brisk* pace, subtract this number from your proper exercising pulse rate. Then, extend your walks five minutes for every ten beats per minute you fall below the standard. It's easy. Say your proper exercise pulse is 150 beats per minute, but you can only get your heart rate up to 135 beats per minute, no matter how fast you walk. In this case, you must add seven and one-half minutes to your consecutive 12 minute time period in order to exercise sufficiently. That's eight minutes to warm up, seven and one-half minutes to make up, and 12 minutes to complete your exercise: 27 minutes in all. Do it.

CHAPTER 5

Taking Your Pulse

Before I move any further into the program, I think it might be a good time to explain how to take an exercise pulse, since this is the way you will monitor your heart rate while you are walking. No doubt, many of you already know the procedure, but I'm sure there are others who need the instruction. Besides, the old familiar one-minute count and even the newer 15-second count are no longer acceptable. So read through this chapter and practice the method I describe; it is yet another key to successful exercise and another step in understanding the workings of your body.

Of all the arteries that could be used to take your pulse, two stand out because of their locations and because of the strength of their pulsations. The most familiar is the radial artery in the wrist, the one doctors and nurses use when they examine you. The other is the carotid artery in the neck. Either of these is perfectly acceptable for our purposes.

Naturally, the first step in taking a pulse is to locate the artery. The radial runs down the thumb side of the inner wrist in line with the index finger. The carotid courses the front of the neck on either side of the larynx (voice box). Refer to the illustrations and try to identify each of these arteries right now. Become familiar with their locations so you can quickly discover them while you are exercising.

In taking the pulse, place all of the fingers of one hand over the length of the artery, either the radial or the carotid, whichever you think is easier. Utilize all of your fingertips, instead of just one or two, to increase the likelihood of identifying the pulse quickly and easily. Never use your thumb, since it has a detectable pulse of its own that can throw off your count.

Once the beat of the artery is discovered, there are several ways of computing the pulse rate—the number of beats per minute. The old way is to count every pulsation in one full minute or to count the pulsations in 15 seconds and multiply that number by four. However, although these methods give an accurate determination of the pulse rate, they are not suitable for recording your exercise pulse. There's good reason for this.

Whenever you run, swim, or walk, it becomes necessary to stop what you are doing in order to take your pulse. In doing so, that is in discontinuing the exercise, your heart and pulse rates rapidly diminish. For this reason, the one-minute pulse determination, and even the 15-second count, are not indicative of the true exercise pulse, the highest rate achieved during the exercise. Rather, each measures a declining pulse rate.

To overcome this problem, you must take a six-second pulse. Count the number of beats in six seconds, then multiply this number by ten. For example, seven beats in six seconds would be the equivalent of 70 beats per minute, eight beats would be 80 beats per minute, and so on. If you detect slightly more than

TAKING YOUR PULSE

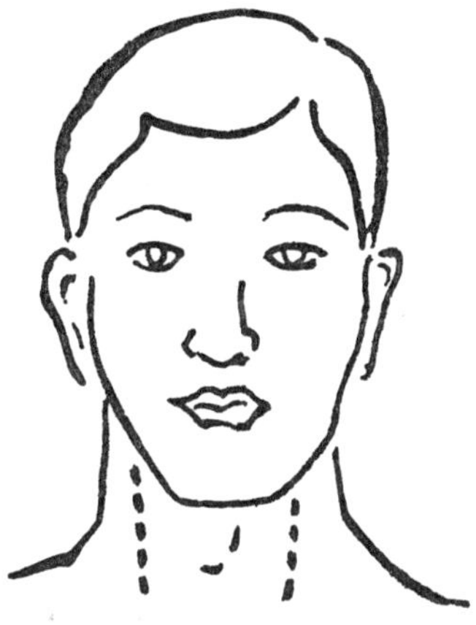

SIX-SECOND PULSE

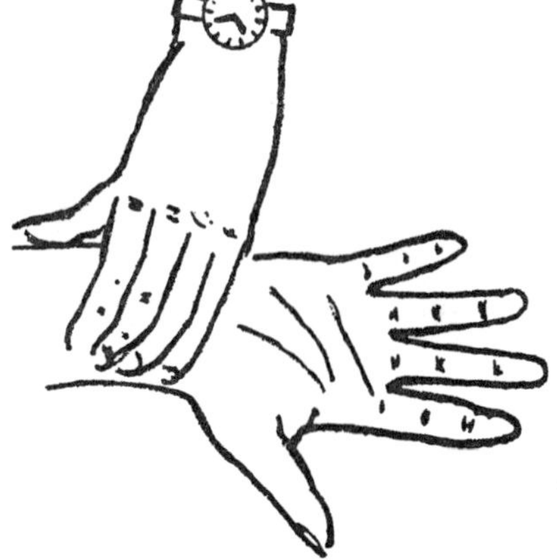

eight beats in six seconds, say eight and a half, simply multiply that number by ten, giving 85 beats per minute.

You can try it right now with your resting pulse. Although some people will get readings as low as four beats in six seconds, others may record as many as ten. You should count approximately eight, which would be about average and would compute out to a pulse rate of 80 beats per minute. However, if you do get a resting pulse of 65 (six and a half beats in six seconds) or below, refer back to page 00 in the last chapter and reread the special note for people with low resting pulses.

During periods of exercise, your pulse rate will be significantly elevated over your resting standard. In fact, as I explained in the previous chapter, it must be maintained at 75 percent of the maximum heart rate for your age if you expect to improve your physical condition. Consequently, you should monitor your pulse regularly, especially when you start the program, to make sure you are exercising properly. Once you become familiar with your new routine, this won't be necessary. Instead, you can take your pulse at the beginning and at the end of the important 12 consecutive minutes of nonstop walking that comprises the core of the walking program, just to see if you have exercised in your specific aerobic target zone.

By pulse-monitoring your physical activity, after your warming-up and again before your cooling-off period, regardless of whether you are walking, swimming, or running, you can be assured that you are exercising at the proper pace. You will also insure the well-being of your heart and guarantee your chances to live and exercise another day. All things considered, it's the intelligent approach to exercise.

Now let's move on to the important warming-up and cooling-off periods.

CHAPTER 6

Warming up—Cooling off

The phrases "warming up" and "cooling off" may or may not be familiar to you. Respectively, they indicate a gradual increase and gradual decrease in physical activity—interims between the resting state and periods of vigorous exertion. Both are important components of a balanced, well-designed exercise program and deserve individual consideration to prepare you for walking.

Warming up

I have been asked many times, "Exactly how important is a warm-up and is it really necessary before pulse-monitored walking?"

Well, let me clear the air about this once and for all.

A warm-up is a very important part of any exercise and is absolutely required before aerobic walking.

By raising the temperature of the body gradually, warm-ups prevent injury to muscles (including your heart muscle), tendons, and ligaments. Warmed muscles will contract with greater force and speed when called upon to work harder. And proper warm-ups will also delay the fatigue and increase the endurance that results from more vigorous activity. Since aerobic walking is significantly strenuous and involves over 50 percent of all the muscles of the body, an adequate warm-up is always needed.

Now the question arises: What constitutes a proper walking warm-up?

Basically, there are two kinds of warm-ups—those that are related to the anticipated exercise (related warm-ups) and those that are not (unrelated warm-ups). For example, a warm-up related to aerobic walking would be strolling or slow non-aerobic walking whereby you perform a physical activity that is similar to the planned exercise of vigorous walking. An example of an unrelated warm-up would be toe touches or deep knee bends. While these exercises do not directly mimic the muscular contractions that characterize walking, they do warm the body and stretch some of the individual muscle groups that will ultimately be employed when you walk. In this sense they help to prepare your body for the more strenuous exertion.

Both related and unrelated warm-ups are good, but I personally believe that related warm-ups are more effective because they involve the exact same muscle groups as the primary exercise. Therefore, as part of the walking program, I recommend that you perform the related activity of strolling in preparation for the aerobic segment of your walk.

By starting off slowly, and gradually increasing your walking pace until you have reached your aerobic target zone—75 percent of your maximum pulse rate—you will be assured of adequately warming up your body, your heart and lungs, plus all of your muscles, for the more strenuous exertion that occurs during the aerobic segment of your walk. During your warm-up, you can perform the upper body walking exercises that I will teach you in Chapter 12, but they are totally optional. Your main concern is to gradually increase your activity for approximately eight minutes and slowly raise your heart rate to the correct exercising level. Once you have reached this level, you must then sustain that pulse rate for at least twelve consecutive nonstop minutes in order to obtain the full aerobic benefit from your walk. Following the aerobic segment, you must cool off before ending the exercise session.

Cooling off

Whereas the warm-up prepares you for more strenuous activity, the cooling-off period prepares you for rest or a cessation of the exercise. This, too, is an important part of the walking program; far more important than even the warm-up.

You see, while you are walking, the blood vessels of the legs and hips widen in order to supply the working muscles with more blood and oxygen. As the muscles contract with each of your strides, blood is forcefully pumped back to the heart like water being squeezed out of a sponge. Subsequently, this blood is reoxygenated and then recirculated back to the leg muscles.

Now what do you think would happen if you suddenly stopped walking?

Well, your heart would continue to beat at an accelerated rate for a few minutes, trying to fill the heated muscles with blood. And your breathing would continue to be slightly labored in an attempt to provide the oxygen your exercised body desperately needs. But since you are no longer walking, the muscles of your legs are no longer contracting and your blood is not being adequately pumped back to your heart. Instead, it remains pooled in your legs. Consequently, your blood pressure declines abruptly, and your vital organs experience a temporary insufficiency in blood flow. While some people can compensate adequately for this inappropriate distribution of blood, others cannot. Dizziness, fainting, nausea, and vomiting can result. More significantly, heart attack and stroke can occur. Obviously, these hazards must be avoided. You can avert them successfully with a proper cooling-off period.

By slowly decreasing the intensity of your walking and gradually allowing your leg muscles to cool off, you will prevent the uneven distribution of blood that can occur in the post-exercise state. This is the objective of the cooling-off period. Actually, it is a reversal of the warm-up.

Following the aerobic segment of your walk, you must maintain some activity for at least five minutes. I advise slow walking or strolling, combined with those walking exercises that stress the lower extremities (Chapter 12). These cooling-off procedures will allow the body to revert back to normal temperature slowly while adequate blood flow is maintained. They will also help to rid the leg muscles of waste products and toxins that have accumulated during the exercise.

It is tremendously important that you exercise to stay well. And it is wise to walk, since walking is the safest and most natural exercise you can perform. But do it intelligently. Always pulse-monitor your activity, and start your exercise with a gradual warm-up and end it with a slow cooling-off period. By following these simple techniques, you will get the most benefit from your exercise sessions, and you will preserve your well-being while you are exercising.

CHAPTER 7

Before the Program

In the United States, heart disease is the most common cause of death among adults; it kills almost one million Americans each year. Unfortunately for males, they are stricken more frequently than females, and at an earlier age. In fact, among men between the ages of 35 and 55, over 50,000 will die from heart disease this year alone, and countless more will live debilitated lives in the aftermath of a cardiac calamity. Among the female population in the same age span, about 15,000 will die and, of course, thousands more will survive but suffer. In an older population, 55 to 75 years of age, about 200,000 men and 100,000 women will succumb to heart disease, and beyond age 75, about 350,000 combined deaths will occur this year. These figures seem very high, don't you think, especially since heart disease is highly preventable in the younger adult population: that is, among men and women between the ages of 35 and 75.

Positively, with a knowledge of the predisposing factors and a determination to protect yourself, you can live longer without the fear of a heart attack.

Of all the risk factors leading to cardiac disease, lack of exercise is foremost. This fact had been confirmed over and over again by independent researchers in different parts of the world; it is undeniable. High blood pressure, diabetes, obesity, anxiety, heredity, and high-fat diets are still other predisposing factors. Among them all, your heredity is the only thing you cannot change. If your mother or father, your grandmother or grandfather dies of a heart attack or another heart problem, your chances of developing a similar problem are increased, but still highly controllable.

While the beginnings of heart disease evidently develop at an early age, possibly even during adolescence, as we now know, men over 35 and postmenopausal women over 55 run the greatest danger of serious heart problems like heart attacks. This danger can be greatly diminished with a sensible diet and a routine exercise program. However, it is not uncommon for people to actually suffer heart attacks while exercising, especially if they fail to gauge the intensity of their activity or forget to obtain medical clearance before starting their exercise program, which brings us to the point of this chapter. The best way for you to determine your potential risk of exercise-induced injury is to have a physical examination and stress EKG prior to initiating your walking regimen.

While walking is the safest of all exercises, I'm sure there will be someone who tries to do too much too soon. And if just one of you suffers a heart attack after entering my program, although this is highly unlikely, I would feel terrible. So please follow my recommendations as to who should see a doctor before starting this or any other exercise routine. Personally, this is so important to me that I have made it one of my *Ten Walking Rules* and have even labeled it with a warning. The rule is:

> WARNING: All men over 40 and all postmenopausal women should see their doctors before beginning any exercise program.

If you fit into either of these two categories, that is, if you are a male over 40 or a postmenopausal woman, you owe it to yourself to have a regular yearly checkup anyway. During your examination, you can inform your doctor about your desire to exercise and, at the same time, request a stress EKG. In this way, your doctor can confirm your good health and also give his personal endorsement to my program. I'm sure he will encourage you.

On the other hand, if you are a man under forty or a premenopausal woman, it is probably unnecessary for you to see your doctor, unless you have a known medical problem that requires his attention. You can start the program immediately as long as your answer to all of the following questions is "no."

PRE-EXERCISE CHECKOUT LIST

1. Were you ever told that you had rheumatic fever, scarlet fever, or rheumatic heart disease?
2. Have you ever had a heart murmur?
3. Do you have any known or suspected heart trouble?
4. During physical or sexual activity, have you ever suffered from chest pain or a pressure sensation in your chest that might extend into your neck or left shoulder?
5. Have you ever had angina pectoris, otherwise known as simple angina?

6. Have you ever taken nitroglycerin pills which are placed under your tongue to relieve chest pain?
7. Have you ever taken any other drugs for your heart?
8. Do you develop extreme shortness of breath when climbing stairs?
9. Have you ever had an abnormal electrocardiogram (EKG, ECG)?
10. Do you ever become confused or become dizzy and light-headed when trying to exercise?
11. Do you ever become very weak, possibly unsteady, with physical exertion?
12. Do your lips, fingers, or face become pale or purplish when you exercise?
13. Does your heart ever beat irregularly or unexpectedly pound in your chest?
14. Have you ever been told you have high blood pressure or hypertension?
15. Have you ever been given "water pills" for your blood pressure?
16. Have people in your family suffered heart attacks at an early age?
17. Are you 25 pounds overweight?
18. Have you ever been placed on a low fat, low cholesterol diet?
19. Have you ever had abnormal lab tests for fat or cholesterol in your blood?
20. Have you ever taken medication to lower your cholesterol?
21. Have you ever had diabetes?
22. Do you have an abnormal sugar content in your blood or urine?
23. Have you ever had asthma, emphysema, or other lung disease?
24. Do you get cramping pains in your legs or calves when you walk?

If you have answered "yes" to any of the previous questions, you should see your doctor and inform him of your intention to exercise. These questions do reveal potential hazards and deserve medical attention at the beginning of this or any other exercise program.

If you have answered "no" to all of the above questions, you are probably in fairly good health; surely, you are ready for brisk walking. By applying yourself to the walking program conscientiously, hopefully you will never answer "yes" to these questions or any others like them.

DURING

With an awareness of the problem and a desire to make a change, you can implement a solution. But you must have the knowledge and means to do so.

You already have the means, your own two feet, now you must learn how to use them properly.

CHAPTER 8

Warning Signals

Not only must you be aware of your pre-existing medical problems before you start my program, you should also be alert to some of the potential hazards you might encounter along the way. To prevent any catastrophes, it is important that you follow all of the instructions I have provided in this book. This particularly applies to monitoring your pulse while you walk, for it is your essential guide to successful exercising. In practice, if you find that your pulse is below the proper exercise level, you will have to walk faster. On the other hand, if it is too high, you will have to slow down. Frequent pulse monitoring at the start of the program will not only assure your well-being, it will also guarantee excellent conditioning results.

But you must also realize that although you correctly maintain your proper exercise pulse, it is possible, though unlikely, for you to overexert yourself while walking. This particularly applies to the elderly and those with pre-existing medical problems. You see, at any given time, unanticipated conditions can place undue stress on your body and cause trouble, even though you are exercising properly.

For example, on a particularly hot day you might overburden your cardiovascular system and suffer from heat exhaustion. When it is extremely cold, you might have trouble breathing and fail to keep up with your increased oxygen needs. Then, too, it is possible that the average exercising heart rate for your age is too much for you to handle. Therefore, it is imperative that you use your own bodily sense and good judgement on a daily basis to detect any of the problems that might arise while you walk.

To help you recognize these potential dangers, I will now describe the medical signs and symptoms of common exercising ailments. If you notice any of them during your walks, you should curtail your activity and follow the instructions I have provided for each case. Don't be frightened; there's no need for alarm. But it is important that you consult your doctor, when indicated, or apply the remedy I suggest.

Certainly, the most significant warning you should heed during any exercise is chest pain. Although the pain may be felt on the surface of the chest, with possible extension into your left arm or neck, it may actually originate in your heart. And while its presence does not necessarily mean you are having a heart attack, it does indicate some form of cardiac stress that requires immediate attention. Accordingly, all exercise should be stopped, and a consultation with your doctor should be obtained as soon as possible. Also note, this pain may occur some time after your walk, and, in such cases, still necessitates a call to the doctor.

Additional heart warning symptoms which you may detect in

your pulse include palpitations, irregular heart beats, a fluttering pulse, or a rapid fall in your pulse that is extreme and unexpected. Again, these symptoms may occur during your walks or shortly thereafter. They should be brought to the attention of your doctor.

Other signs of trouble that should be regarded with suspicion include dizziness or light-headedness, plus lack of coordination and a cold clammy sweat. Although these symptoms probably don't indicate a heart condition, they still require attention because they do suggest a decrease in blood flow to the brain that could lead to fainting and collapse. Consequently, if you notice them while you are walking, stop, and sit down with your head between your legs if possible, or lie on your back, whichever is more comfortable. Remain calm for a few minutes, then when the symptoms clear, proceed home slowly. Be sure to discuss the incident with your doctor before your next walk.

Again, most of the above symptoms should be uncommon, especially among young walkers. However, older individuals and those with pre-existing medical problems may at times notice them. Don't be alarmed or panic if they occur, but definitely follow through in having them checked out.

More common problems that anyone might experience while walking, include strains, sprains, and cramps in the feet and legs. They predominantly occur when muscles that are out of shape are exercised too vigorously, and, although these ailments may be painful, they are usually insignificant and easily treated.

For ordinary cramping, stop your walk and massage the affected muscle until it relaxes. Relief should occur within a few minutes. However, if the crampy pain is due to insufficient blood flow to your legs, a condition known as claudication, relief may be more difficult to obtain, and the problem will probably recur. You see, unlike the simple cramping that results from muscle fatigue, claudication is caused by a buildup of atherosclerotic plaque in the arteries of the legs. As the plaque accumulates, it slowly plugs the arteries and gradually restricts the vital flow of blood. Under ordinary inactive conditions, you might not notice the change or perceive any problem, but when you exert yourself by walking and increase the oxygen and blood requirement in your leg muscles, crampy pain develops because of inadequate blood flow. Therefore, I advise you to see your doctor under these more severe and persistent circumstances.

Less significant than claudication yet more troublesome than ordinary cramping, strains and sprains of the foot and lower leg also require attention, but these you can handle yourself. Initially they call for ice packs around the affected area to prevent swelling and extension of injury. Later you can apply hot water soaks for healing and take aspirin or aspirin substitutes for pain.

The ice should be applied at 20 minute intervals, that's twenty minutes on and 20 minutes off, as many times as possible during the first day of injury. Then, from the second day onward, the hot water soaks and pain relievers are recommended. Also, an Ace bandage can be applied for support. With this therapy, you should be better in a few days, at which time you can resume your walking. But next time remember: most muscle, tendon, and ligament problems can be totally avoided barring any unforeseen accidents with the proper warm-up. So try to prevent these injuries with a gradual increase in your walking pace and you won't have to treat them.

While on the subject of muscle problems, I should mention a special cramp called the diaphragmatic spasm, otherwise known as the "side stitch." I am sure you have experienced it before while walking, running, or possibly during some other form of physical activity. It consists of a sharp pain under the rib cage and results when the muscles of the diaphragm, those that are used for breathing, become crampy and spastic with exercise. Since it is fairly common among walkers, be prepared if it occurs and follow the upcoming instructions for relief. As your fitness improves, the likelihood of occurence is reduced.

Upon first noticing the pain, you should stop walking and take a few slow deep breaths, exhaling completely, hoping the diaphragm relaxes and the pain subsides. If it doesn't, look for a comfortable place to sit down and rest. Then, while in the sitting position, lean forward and push up on your abdomen with your hands. Breathing slowly while in this position, empty the lungs totally of air for a few seconds. Repeat the procedure a few times if necessary. After a couple of minutes and a little relaxation, the spasm will clear and you can continue on your journey. But go slowly at first to prevent a recurrence of this symptom.

Other less likely problems you might incur on your walks include nausea, vomiting, and excessive fatigue. Although these symptoms are usually associated with more strenuous exercises, like jogging and swimming, because of their extreme demand for oxygen, they may also occur with walking. However, in this case, they usually indicate the presence of some unrelated ailment, such as a cold, the flu, or gastroenteritis. By reducing your walking pace, they may spontaneously disappear. But if they persist and are associated with additional signs of illness, see your doctor and resume your walking program when you feel better. Exercising while you are ill is not recommended because your body will not be able to benefit from the activity and you will only aggravate the existing ailment.

Those of you who suffer from arthritis, bursitis, or gout may notice a flare-up of these problems when you exercise. The vigorous movement of your joints may break up small areas of fibrous scarring and may lead to some temporary discomfort. Since you have experienced them before, you probably know what to do about them, and I suggest you treat them as you normally would. Aspirin or aspirin substitutes should relieve the pain, and heat applied to the affected area should aid healing. After a few days of rest, you should be able to resume your walking program. But don't overdo it at first. Gradually work back to your preceeding intensity and distance, thus giving the affected joints a chance to fully recuperate before vigoriously stressing them again.

CHAPTER 9

Breathing

One of the most important aspects of aerobic exercise is regular deep breathing . . . something most people rarely do.

Yogis and those familiar with oriental culture and practice call it Pranayama, the Science of Breath. They have studied and practiced respiratory control for centuries and believe that the life force in our bodies is controlled by the act of breathing, the most critical of all bodily functions. They look at it this way: as the infant takes its first breath and proclaims its birth with a long wail, life begins. As the elder gives up his will and the air flows quietly from his lungs for the last time, life as we know it ends. From the first breath to the last, life is sustained through the ceaseless act of breathing. And in this sense, as the yogis put it, truly, "Breath is life." But there's more to it than that.

They believe that correct breathing habits will provide continued vitality and freedom from disease. Through breath control, they say, our lives will be lengthened and enriched—physically, mentally, and spiritually. And with correct breathing practices we can extend a flow of vital force, Prana, to any part of our body, thereby increasing the strength and vitality of any organ or limb. Better health, greater concentration, happiness, self-control, clear-sightedness, and a stronger sense of morality are the rewards.

Those of you who have studied yoga or have taken yoga classes may already be familiar with these thoughts. Perhaps you have even practiced breath control with an instructor. For those of you who are unfamiliar with these teachings, I mention them here only to provide greater insight into the importance of proper breathing on all our body functions, especially during periods of exercise.

You see, the yogis have formed a complete science around the act of breathing and have studied the phenomenon for centuries. In so doing, they have directed their full concentration on every muscular contraction and the slightest of chest movements involved in respiration. Truly, they are the masters. In addition, they have also created a rich spiritualism around Breath and Pranayama, the Science of Breath. I find this spiritualism, this allusion to something greater, can provide inspiration to the exerciser and create an awareness for the body magic that results from deep breathing.

For example, Oriental teachings state that rhythmical breathing brings one into harmonious vibration with nature and aids in the development or expression of latent powers. While this may sound nebulous and philosophic, it is easily confirmed through experience. Perhaps a case in point will prove enlightening.

Six years ago, I was fortunate enough to spend some time

with a good friend, Peter Miller. Peter and I had been exercising one morning—push-ups and sit-ups—and decided to go for a walk and a jog. As we stomped around the streets of Pompano Beach, our pace was moderate and relaxed, but I noticed that Peter was becoming quite winded. Observing his breathing technique, I quickly realized he had none; he was breathing spontaneously, but erratically and shallowly. When I called this to his attention and suggested that he inhale deeply on four paces and exhale completely on four paces, his breathing became much more regular and efficient because it was timed with his jogging rhythm. In a short while Peter was breathing more comfortably although he was still exercising at the same pace. Obviously, the rhythmical breathing brought him greater endurance, greater power.

The same principal of breath control applies to all physical activity. The weight lifter who coordinates his breathing with his maneuvers will realize greater strength and will be able to lift more weight. The swimmer who successfully learns the correct method of breathing between strokes can swim further with less effort. And the walker who concentrates on matching his breathing with his strides will likewise achieve the benefits of breath control, during the exercise and continuously thereafter.

To better comprehend the correct methods of breathing we must understand the mechanics of respiration, the muscular movements that allow air to flow into and out of our lungs. With this knowledge comes a greater appreciation of what the yogis call "complete breathing" and a greater sense of breath control. Let's start with inhalation.

As the chest expands during inhalation a momentary vacuum is created and air rushes into the lungs. However, it is not the lungs, themselves, that cause the air to flow. It is the movement of the respiratory muscles, the diaphragm and the intercostals, that is responsible. These individual muscle groups, by expanding specific areas of the chest, create the vacuum and produce the influx of air. The lungs simply react passively.

Various patterns of breathing have, in fact, been named for the different contractions that characterize them. No doubt you have heard of diaphragmatic breathing, also known as abdominal breathing, which results from the lowering of the diaphragm and the extension of the abdomen. Intercostal breathing, on the other hand, refers to the breath that is produced by the contraction of the intercostal muscles which are located between the ribs. And clavicular breathing accounts for the air movement that occurs when the collarbones, the clavicles, are muscularly elevated during a breath. While each of these individual patterns successfully causes inhalation, they are all incomplete in and of themselves and only partially fill the lungs with air.

As simple and basic as breathing is, surprisingly, few people breathe correctly. Due to our sedentary lives, there is little need for full breathing; we rarely exert ourselves enough to require it. Consequently, shallow incomplete breathing predominates our respiratory patterns, and much of the time the lungs are in a collapsed state. As a result, lung disease has become more and more prominent, drooping shoulders and sunken chests are very common, and a host of related medical problems, like backaches and fatigue, plague our daily lives.

To correct these maladies, the yogis have devised a method of complete breathing. Their intent: to fill the lungs completely, to stretch and expand them to their fullest capacity, and in so doing, to intensify and control the Prana, the power, that is inherent in each breath. For them, a complete breath is actually a combination of the three forms of incomplete breathing previously described. They utilize abdominal breathing to fill the lower lobes of the lungs. Then focus on intercostal breathing to inflate the middle lungs. And finish the breath with clavicular breathing, thereby filling the upper lobes. Generally speaking, the breathing patterns of inactive incomplete breathers only fall into one of these three categories, and as I have mentioned, fail to produce a complete breath.

In order to fully understand the nature of a complete breath, try the following exercise.

1. Sit or stand erect and exhale completely.
2. Breathing through the nostrils, inhale slowly but deeply and fill the lower lobes of your lungs by extending your abdomen which will pull your diaphragm downward.
3. As you reach the limits of this abdominal or diaphragmatic breathing, slowly shift emphasis to your rib cage, pushing the ribs and breastbone outward, expanding the chest forward. Air will flow into the middle lobes.
4. Now, as you reach the limits of your chest expansion, attempt to elevate your entire rib cage and shoulders, shifting emphasis again, this time to the upper chest. By lifting the chest and raising the clavicles, you will fill the upper lobes of each lung and complete the last part of a full breath.

When performed properly, the complete breath is accomplished with one continuous movement, not three separate actions. Try it a few times until you get the feel of it.

By breathing deeply, the yogis say there are countless improvements to overall health. Since the vitality of the lungs is greatly improved, respiratory tissue is better able to resist the invasion of bacteria and viruses. Consequently, the incidence of colds, flus, and pneumonias is dramatically reduced, and tuberculosis becomes virtually nonexistent.

The quality of the blood is likewise improved by the increase in aeration. And, the entire body, each and every organ plus all the muscles, benefits from the life-giving oxygen.

Furthermore, the stomach and the other organs of digestion are gently massaged by the up and down movement of the diaphragm. As a result, their actions are enhanced because food is propelled along with greater facility, and blood is more effectively pumped into and out of these organs.

By this time you might be thinking I have forgotten all about the topic of this chapter—walking and breathing. But I assure you, it has been on my mind constantly. I just wanted to present my case for walking in a different light, hoping you would come to better appreciate its true value. You see, I believe all those things the yogis say about breathing deeply. How it rejuvenates and stimulates the entire body. How it prevents disease and prolongs life. Only I see no need for the deep breathing exercises they prescribe. If each of us would walk every day for just one-half hour, we would realize all of the benefits of deep breathing, only we would achieve them in a much more natural way, doing the exercise for which our bodies were intended, walking. Not only that, we would derive all of the aerobic benefits as well—the expansion of our capillary network, the stimulation of our enzyme systems, the exercise to our heart, the utilization of calories, all those wonderful things that result from increasing our oxygen needs and filling those needs by breathing deeply while walking.

Now I am not overlooking or contradicting the wisdom of the Oriental teachers; I think there's much to learn from their thoughts. I merely advocate the natural combination of deep breathing with walking as the best means of achieving the much desired end results, the greater power and endurance, the excellent physical and mental health, that both easterners and westerners seek.

If you walk aerobically as I have instructed, you will notice that your breathing automatically becomes deeper because you create a greater need for oxygen in your body and must fill that need by breathing deeply. Once you realize this, it is up to you to augment each breath. The important thing to remember is: you must coordinate your breathing with your strides and concentrate on taking a full complete breath with each inspiration. This should be your approach.

Using the cadence of your footsteps to regulate your breathing, I want you to perform a yogi complete breath, as described earlier in the chapter, on the count of eight. That is, on your first foot strike, count number one, employ the diaphragmatic breathing I described earlier to start off the inhalation, filling the lower lobes of your lungs. On count number four, your fourth foot strike, use your intercostal muscle, those located between your ribs, to expand your chest and carry the inhalation. On your sixth foot strike, count number six, complete the expansion of your lungs. Then finish the inhalation at eight with a complete clavicular breath. Hold your breath for a second then begin to slowly exhale on the next count of eight, your next eight footsteps. Make each inhalation long and smooth, filling your lungs to capacity each time. Exhale in a similar fashion.

If you find that the count of eight is unsuited to your particular respiratory needs, inhale on a count of four, or six, or ten, whatever feels right. Regardless, the intent is to use all of your respiratory muscles and all of your available lung space as you walk and breathe. Alter your breathing rhythm to coordinate it with your walking stride as your need for oxygen changes during your walk. Beware of hyperventilation.

Experiment with yourself until your particular pattern develops, then use it religiously. By following this method, you will realize all of the benefits of deep breathing—all of the things the yogis have discovered through centuries of study and reflection. Truly, this method of combining deep breathing and walking is the most efficient and practical way of perfecting one's health. It is, in fact, the best of both worlds.

CHAPTER 10

When and Where

Now you're ready to create your own walking schedule with a little help from me. First you must decide on a time and a place that is in keeping with your natural daily patterns. Then you must make walking a way of life, an integral part of daily living, using the schedule you have created. In a short period of time, walking will develop into a distinct daily pleasure, something that is enjoyed like fine champagne. For if it is a drudgery or a forced affair, you won't enjoy it and you'll never stick with it. So read the suggestions and alternatives that follow and select for yourself those walking patterns that fit your particular lifestyle. I know for some of you, variety is the key to a successful walking program. For others, a fixed daily routine is the only sure approach. Regardless, the choice is yours, so read, walk, and enjoy.

When

Unlike all other exercises or sports, walking has absolutely no time limitations. Any time you can spare is well spent. If you have only 15 minutes, you can walk a mile. Certainly, if you were to run or swim a mile every day, you would be proud of your accomplishment. Well, here's an easier and better way . . . walking. The important thing to remember is that you must take the time to walk daily. You must follow your walking schedule.

Basically, there are two components to a good schedule.

First, you must reserve a daily 30-minute time slot that is utilized solely for walking. Be sensible and choose a time that fits comfortably into your day—a time that feels right.

You might choose to walk in the mornings before preparing for work, or maybe at lunchtime when the rigors of a brisk walk will freshen you for the afternoon's labors. Perhaps a walk before or after dinner is more appealing to you. Whatever time you choose, however, stick with it and try not to miss a single day, not even one. By developing a set routine and maintaining a rigid schedule, your walks will become second nature to you—a beneficial habit if you will—and this should be one of your major objectives. So remember, choose a time that's compatible with your other activities and stick with it, every day.

Here's a helpful suggestion.

Initially, if you have trouble choosing the ideal time period, experiment with yourself until you come up with the right formula. Eventually you'll discover the times that are best for you. At first you might ask yourself: When is a walk most convenient? When will it be most enjoyable? When is it most needed? By answering these questions and rotating your schedule accordingly, you will ultimately create the proper program for your individual needs. Although you might have two or three acceptable time periods set aside each day, you need to utilize only one of them, the best one for that particular occasion. In this way, your schedule will provide variety and still impose daily control. I think this method is the most intelligent approach.

The second component of an effective walking schedule is spontaneity. Not only must you set aside 30 minutes each day for your routine walks, you must also take advantage of every other walking opportunity that presents itself to you, anytime, day or night. You must walk more at work, and that doesn't simply mean walking to and from the escalator and elevator or from one desk to another. It means walking up and down the stairs, across the street to the printer, down the road to the post office, and around the block to that business meeting. By scheduling your time wisely, you can perform much of your daily travel on foot and improve your overall level of health and fitness at the same time.

You must also walk more at home, before and after work. Opportunities abound if you can break the habit of jumping into your car every time you must run an errand or visit a friend. You'll be saving more than just gasoline if you do all of your traveling on foot; you'll be saving your life!

Whenever you walk, at home or at work, always apply the principles I have taught you. Although a five-minute walking errand won't provide the benefit of a full twelve-minute aerobic walk, with its warming-up and cooling-off periods, you will still be getting great exercise, burning off calories, stimulating your heart and lungs, and limbering your muscles. At the same time, you will be completing some task or errand that might otherwise have been nothing more than a drudgery. Truly, walking errands are the most selfserving means of mixing business and pleasure.

Where

It may seem a little strange that I am telling you where to walk, especially since you know more about your neighborhood than I do. But for quite some time I have searched out the likely as well as the unlikely spots that are ideal for walking. In the process, I have found that many excellent locations and opportunities are frequently overlooked and seldom utilized. Maybe in describing them to you, I can focus your attention on similar situations where you live and work. Combined with the numerous walking locations you already know, you should have hundreds of potential walkways to choose from.

Actually, any pleasant place is sufficient, but locations that accommodate daily tasks and usual travel are, of course, best. When you go to work in the morning, find a walking path that will take you at least part of the way there. If you must commute because of distance, walk to the train, then get off a few blocks early. Walk past two or three bus stops and end your ride sooner than usual. Do the same with the subway. If you must drive, you can park your car many blocks from your destination and walk the remaining distance. Walk to and from lunch. Walk home after work or reverse the process that got you to work.

Those of you who spend the day at home will probably find few opportunities and locations to walk during the day. Unfortunately, many of our residential neighborhoods are ill-designed for walking and our suburbs are so spread out. Then, too, mothers with children have the added responsibility and restriction of raising the family. But believe me, you are the people who need walking the most . . . all of you.

Young mothers who get so wound up trying to watch the kids, do the laundry, clean the house, cook the food, and take care of Dad when he gets home truly need a mini-vacation during the day—a little time to be alone and unwind. After bending over to clean the floors and fighting the morning and afternoon traffic taking the kids to and from school, you need to stretch your legs and soothe your nerves.

You'll find that within a half hour of walking you'll feel like new again, ready to face the next battery of family demands and social responsibilities. Since your job is never-ending, you must make the time to walk and relax. You must do it every day.

You older folks who spend most of your time indoors, reading and watching television, you're all in physical jeopardy and you know it. You've felt your joints stiffen and witnessed your muscles fade away. But you don't do anything about it. You say you're bored and lonely and you'd like to make new friends, but you'll never change your life just sitting on the sofa all day. You've got to get out and walk.

For you, walking will be a stimulant to elevate your mood, a gentle massage to soothe your aching bones, and a personal encounter with other people like yourself. It will make you look and feel ten years younger. But you must do it religiously, not just a few times each month.

And let's not forget about the home-based men. All you guys who are getting round instead of robust. You fellows who play one afternoon of softball and can't move for a week. With blood pressure rates as high as your new mortgage rates, you need to walk as much as anyone else . . . to be alone and think out your problems step by step, to relax. Or maybe you need to clear your thoughts with a quick pace and a lot of fresh air. Regardless, you'll find that walking does it all and, at the same time, puts things back into perspective so that you can make rational judgments with a fresh mental attitude.

Well now, where can all you homebodies walk?

Young mothers can always take the baby for a walk around the neighborhood. But in these instances, the walking pace is usually slower than what I would normally recommend. It would certainly be better to leave the baby with your husband before or after dinner, or maybe with your neighbor for 30 minutes during the day. In this way, you will have the time to be by yourself, to be free to exercise properly and cater to your own physical and mental needs. When you return home, your attitude will be improved and your chores will seem much less troublesome.

When you are running errands in your car or going shopping, look for a park, a playground, or simply a quaint street or neighborhood where you can leave your car for 30 minutes and walk. There should be hundreds of likely places that you overlook every day. Schools, parks, college campuses. Small local airports, golf courses, nurseries. Lakes, rivers, beaches. Use your eyes and take the opportunity to walk every time you come across a new place. After walking, resume your regular affairs; do the shopping or pick up the kids. People will be amazed at your constant vigor and cheerfulness.

And here's a real bonus.

You know those giant malls that have sprung up throughout our suburbs. Well, they all make excellent walking locations, and there's probably one near you.

On pleasant days when you are going shopping at one of these modern megamarkets, you should park your car in the distant reaches of the mall's vast parking lot, as far from the stores as possible. Just walking from your car to the mall is good exercise in itself, but you can take it one step further. Before going inside, walk around the outside of the mall at least one time. In circling the exterior, you may clip off half a mile, maybe more. Then, once you are inside, keep up a healthy pace and walk past all the stores, up and down the stairs, around the entire interior. This may well add another half mile to your walk and bring your total walking distance to more than a mile. Your entire walking time should surely exceed 12 minutes, which means you've done your walking for the day.

Now you are ready to shop. You've seen all the stores so you know what's on sale and where all the bargains are. And you've gotten all the daily exercise you need, without even trying. Two bargains in one.

Well, there you have it; certainly enough suggestions to keep you busy for a while, and enough diversion to offset the potential boredom of routine exercise. But there is one more location that is truly ideal for walking—a place that is literally made for exercising—the track at your local elementary school, high school or college. Most of the time it will be empty and waiting for you. Sometimes you'll come across a few joggers.

In the past, tracks were rarely used, lying in wait for Spring and the school's track team. Then came the joggers and the runners who put these facilities to better use. Now enter the walkers—you and the hundreds of thousands of people like you who want to exercise intelligently.

You'll find that the track provides a safe and well-marked area that is ideal for walking. There's plenty of room and a variety of exercisers. So use your local tracks whenever possible. They're great.

CHAPTER 11

The Program

Now you are ready to enter the walking program. The main objective is to incorporate more walking into your day—to walk whenever possible. This objective can be accomplished in two ways.

First, you should use walking as a major form of transportation. Forget the car, eliminate the bus, avoid the subway, escape the elevator, and use your own two feet to get around. A walk of 20 blocks is a snap, and you can do it much more easily than you'd ever imagine, but first you have to try.

Traveling on foot, you can commute to and from work, if not all of the way, at least part of the way. You can walk the kids to school instead of driving them there. You can even perform daily tasks, such as shopping, completely on foot if you just take the time to plan ahead and schedule your time wisely. With a little reflection, many walking opportunities (see Chapter 10, When and Where) will arise.

Second, you must set aside at least 30 minutes each day that you will use solely for walking. Of course, this can be the time it takes you to walk to work or run an errand during the day, but if you plan on an *additional* half hour of walking during leisure time, you'll really be getting good exercise.

Naturally, whenever you walk, you should walk briskly and elevate your pulse to the correct level of aerobic activity for your age group. Be sure not to saunter or stroll for this type of walking is truly inadequate for your purposes. And don't forget to monitor your pulse to see if your pace is sufficient. If you find that your pulse is too low, you'll have to walk faster. If your pulse is too high, you'll have to slow down. But remember, this is the whole basis of the program so you must become accustomed to it and learn to walk efficiently.

Provided in this chapter is your daily schedule. You must plan ahead and fill in the schedule at least one day in advance. Be sure to set aside your thirty minutes of walking time and mark this on the chart first. Then try to determine, as precisely as possible, all those other times when you might get to walk spontaneously throughout the day (say at lunch) and mark them down too.

Now comes the hard part—you must stick to the schedule, always. You *must* walk during all those time periods you have allotted yourself. In addition, you should walk at all other opportunities.

At the end of each day, fill in any extra time you spent walking but couldn't anticipate. Do not include very short walks around the house or office. But do record all other brisk walks that last for ten consecutive minutes or more. Although these aren't adequate for full aerobic benefit, they still can be accepted because they do provide some physical enhancement. Finally, add up all the time, the total number of minutes that you spent walking that day and complete the chart.

If you come up with 60 minutes of effective walking at the end of each day, you're doing just great. But even if you manage only 12 consecutive minutes at the correct walking pulse level, you have at least gotten your minimum daily allotment.

At the start of the program, I want you to establish your cardiac recovery rate as described in Chapter 15. This initial rate will tell you how fit you are before you begin to improve your health by walking and should be recorded in the chart. At the end of each week, you should repeat the procedure so you have an ongoing record of your progress. Within a month you should start to see an improvement.

In addition to cardiac recovery, you should record your *resting* pulse, blood pressure, and weight. (Blood pressure can be determined using the do-it-yourself blood pressure machines that are found in malls, airports, banks, and many other convenient locations. Normal range is 100 systolic/60 diastolic to 140/90.) By following these four physical signs you will be more aware of your body's fitness and the improvement that results from walking.

If you are in very poor condition, you will notice a marked improvement very quickly. However, if you are only slightly out of shape, the improvement will take a little more time to become apparent. Regardless, you must follow the instructions of this book whenever you walk, and in good time all those aerobic benefits I have discussed will come to you. Hopefully, walking will become an intricate part of your life, something you do without a second thought, and once that occurs, your health will become better in leaps and bounds. You will have an increased vitality by doing something you love to do, not something you have to do. And you will stay well without even trying.

So, begin with your recovery rate, resting pulse, and blood

pressure, add your weight, and go from there. Use the schedule to its full capacity and follow it everyday.

Now here's your schedule and a capsulization of the most important information in the book, the *Ten Walking Rules.*

1. All men over forty and all postmenopausal women, anyone who has a serious medical problem, and anyone who has answered "yes" to just one question in the medical questionaire in Chapter 7 should consult their doctor before starting this, or any other, exercise program.
2. Before you enter the program, determine your resting pulse, blood pressure, weight, and cardiac recovery rate. Keep weekly records.
3. Whenever you walk, you must raise your pulse to 75 percent of your maximum heart rate. Consult Chapter 4 for the heart rate chart and any special information that might pertain to you. Warming-up and cooling-off periods are essential.
4. You must sustain your proper exercising heart rate for at least 12 consecutive minutes.
5. You must monitor your pulse using the special six-second count to make sure you are exercising at the proper pace.
6. If you are going to walk with a companion make sure your levels of fitness and exercising rates are compatible.
7. Always fill in your walking schedule one day in advance and be sure to stick to the times you have allotted yourself.
8. Immediately acknowledge any of the warning signals described in Chapter 8 and promptly seek medical assistance when necessary.
9. Always coordinate your breathing with your walking pace. See Chapter 9.
10. Walk every day, at every opportunity, from this day onward.

MONTH: (FILL IN DATES)

	SUN	MON	TUES	WED	THUR	FRI	SAT
CR							
BP							
RP							
W							
TIME							
	HRS. MINS.	HRS. MINS.	HRS. MINS.	HRS. MINS.	HRS. MINS.	HRS. MINS.	HRS. MINS.

	SUN	MON	TUES	WED	THUR	FRI	SAT
CR							
BP							
RP							
W							
TIME							
	HRS. MINS	HRS. MINS.	HRS. MINS.	HRS. MINS.	HRS. MINS.	HRS. MINS.	HRS. MINS.

	SUN	MON	TUES	WED	THUR	FRI	SAT
CR							
BP							
RP							
W							
TIME							
	HRS. MINS.	HRS. MINS.	HRS. MINS.	HRS. MINS.	HRS. MINS.	HRS. MINS.	HRS. MINS.

	SUN	MON	TUES	WED	THUR	FRI	SAT
CR							
BP							
RP							
W							
TIME							
	HRS. MINS.	HRS. MINS.	HRS. MINS.	HRS. MINS.	HRS. MINS.	HRS. MINS.	HRS. MINS.

	SUN	MON	TUES	WED	THUR	FRI	SAT
CR							
BP							
RP							
W							
TIME							
	HRS. MINS.	HRS. MINS.	HRS. MINS.	HRS. MINS.	HRS. MINS.	HRS. MINS.	HRS. MINS.

RECAPITULATION FOR MONTH: TOTAL TIME: ______ HRS. ______ MINS.

WEIGHT AT BEGINNING OF MONTH: WEIGHT AT END OF MONTH:

CR=CARDIAC RECOVER BP=BLOOD PRESSURE RP=RESTING PULSE W=WEIGHT

MONTH: (FILL IN DATES)

	SUN	MON	TUES	WED	THUR	FRI	SAT
CR							
BP							
RP							
W							
TIME							
	HRS. MINS.	HRS. MINS.	HRS. MINS.	HRS. MINS.	HRS. MINS.	HRS. MINS.	HRS. MINS.

	SUN	MON	TUES	WED	THUR	FRI	SAT
CR							
BP							
RP							
W							
TIME							
	HRS. MINS.	HRS. MINS.	HRS. MINS.	HRS. MINS.	HRS. MINS.	HRS. MINS.	HRS. MINS.

	SUN	MON	TUES	WED	THUR	FRI	SAT
CR							
BP							
RP							
W							
TIME							
	HRS. MINS.	HRS. MINS.	HRS. MINS.	HRS. MINS.	HRS. MINS.	HRS. MINS.	HRS. MINS.

	SUN	MON	TUES	WED	THUR	FRI	SAT
CR							
BP							
RP							
W							
TIME							
	HRS. MINS.	HRS. MINS.	HRS. MINS.	HRS. MINS.	HRS. MINS.	HRS. MINS.	HRS. MINS.

	SUN	MON	TUES	WED	THUR	FRI	SAT
CR							
BP							
RP							
W							
TIME							
	HRS. MINS.	HRS. MINS.	HRS. MINS.	HRS. MINS.	HRS. MINS.	HRS. MINS.	HRS. MINS.

RECAPITULATION FOR MONTH: TOTAL TIME: ______ HRS. ______ MINS.

WEIGHT AT BEGINNING OF MONTH: WEIGHT AT END OF MONTH:

CR=CARDIAC RECOVER BP=BLOOD PRESSURE RP=RESTING PULSE W=WEIGHT

MONTH: (FILL IN DATES)

	SUN	MON	TUES	WED	THUR	FRI	SAT
CR							
BP							
RP							
W							
TIME							
	HRS. MINS.	HRS. MINS.	HRS. MINS.	HRS. MINS.	HRS. MINS.	HRS. MINS.	HRS. MINS.

	SUN	MON	TUES	WED	THUR	FRI	SAT
CR							
BP							
RP							
W							
TIME							
	HRS. MINS.	HRS. MINS.	HRS. MINS.	HRS. MINS.	HRS. MINS.	HRS. MINS.	HRS. MINS.

	SUN	MON	TUES	WED	THUR	FRI	SAT
CR							
BP							
RP							
W							
TIME							
	HRS. MINS.	HRS. MINS.	HRS. MINS.	HRS. MINS.	HRS. MINS.	HRS. MINS.	HRS. MINS.

	SUN	MON	TUES	WED	THUR	FRI	SAT
CR							
BP							
RP							
W							
TIME							
	HRS. MINS.	HRS. MINS.	HRS. MINS.	HRS. MINS.	HRS. MINS.	HRS. MINS.	HRS. MINS.

	SUN	MON	TUES	WED	THUR	FRI	SAT
CR							
BP							
RP							
W							
TIME							
	HRS. MINS.	HRS. MINS.	HRS. MINS.	HRS. MINS.	HRS. MINS.	HRS. MINS.	HRS. MINS.

RECAPITULATION FOR MONTH: TOTAL TIME: ______ HRS. ______ MINS.

WEIGHT AT BEGINNING OF MONTH: WEIGHT AT END OF MONTH:

CR=CARDIAC RECOVER BP=BLOOD PRESSURE RP=RESTING PULSE W=WEIGHT

MONTH: (FILL IN DATES)

	SUN	MON	TUES	WED	THUR	FRI	SAT
CR							
BP							
RP							
W							
TIME							
	HRS. MINS.	HRS. MINS.	HRS. MINS.	HRS. MINS.	HRS. MINS.	HRS. MINS.	HRS. MINS.

	SUN	MON	TUES	WED	THUR	FRI	SAT
CR							
BP							
RP							
W							
TIME							
	HRS. MINS.	HRS. MINS.	HRS. MINS.	HRS. MINS.	HRS. MINS.	HRS. MINS.	HRS. MINS.

	SUN	MON	TUES	WED	THUR	FRI	SAT
CR							
BP							
RP							
W							
TIME							
	HRS. MINS.	HRS. MINS.	HRS. MINS.	HRS. MINS.	HRS. MINS.	HRS. MINS.	HRS. MINS.

	SUN	MON	TUES	WED	THUR	FRI	SAT
CR							
BP							
RP							
W							
TIME							
	HRS. MINS.	HRS. MINS.	HRS. MINS.	HRS. MINS.	HRS. MINS.	HRS. MINS.	HRS. MINS.

	SUN	MON	TUES	WED	THUR	FRI	SAT
CR							
BP							
RP							
W							
TIME							
	HRS. MINS.	HRS. MINS.	HRS. MINS.	HRS. MINS.	HRS. MINS.	HRS. MINS.	HRS. MINS.

RECAPITULATION FOR MONTH: TOTAL TIME: ______ HRS. ______ MINS.

WEIGHT AT BEGINNING OF MONTH: WEIGHT AT END OF MONTH:

CR=CARDIAC RECOVER BP=BLOOD PRESSURE RP=RESTING PULSE W=WEIGHT

MONTH: (FILL IN DATES)

	SUN	MON	TUES	WED	THUR	FRI	SAT
CR							
BP							
RP							
W							
TIME							
	HRS. MINS.	HRS. MINS.	HRS. MINS.	HRS. MINS.	HRS. MINS.	HRS. MINS.	HRS. MINS.

	SUN	MON	TUES	WED	THUR	FRI	SAT
CR							
BP							
RP							
W							
TIME							
	HRS. MINS	HRS. MINS.	HRS. MINS.	HRS. MINS.	HRS. MINS.	HRS. MINS.	HRS. MINS.

	SUN	MON	TUES	WED	THUR	FRI	SAT
CR							
BP							
RP							
W							
TIME							
	HRS. MINS.	HRS. MINS.	HRS. MINS.	HRS. MINS.	HRS. MINS.	HRS. MINS.	HRS. MINS.

	SUN	MON	TUES	WED	THUR	FRI	SAT
CR							
BP							
RP							
W							
TIME							
	HRS. MINS.	HRS. MINS.	HRS. MINS.	HRS. MINS.	HRS. MINS.	HRS. MINS.	HRS. MINS.

	SUN	MON	TUES	WED	THUR	FRI	SAT
CR							
BP							
RP							
W							
TIME							
	HRS. MINS.	HRS. MINS.	HRS. MINS.	HRS. MINS.	HRS. MINS.	HRS. MINS.	HRS. MINS.

RECAPITULATION FOR MONTH: TOTAL TIME: ______ HRS. ______ MINS.

WEIGHT AT BEGINNING OF MONTH: WEIGHT AT END OF MONTH:

CR=CARDIAC RECOVER BP=BLOOD PRESSURE RP=RESTING PULSE W=WEIGHT

MONTH: (FILL IN DATES)

	SUN	MON	TUES	WED	THUR	FRI	SAT
CR							
BP							
RP							
W							
TIME							
	HRS. MINS.	HRS. MINS.	HRS. MINS.	HRS. MINS.	HRS. MINS.	HRS. MINS.	HRS. MINS.

	SUN	MON	TUES	WED	THUR	FRI	SAT
CR							
BP							
RP							
W							
TIME							
	HRS. MINS	HRS. MINS.	HRS. MINS.	HRS. MINS.	HRS. MINS.	HRS. MINS.	HRS. MINS.

	SUN	MON	TUES	WED	THUR	FRI	SAT
CR							
BP							
RP							
W							
TIME							
	HRS. MINS.	HRS. MINS.	HRS. MINS.	HRS. MINS.	HRS. MINS.	HRS. MINS.	HRS. MINS.

	SUN	MON	TUES	WED	THUR	FRI	SAT
CR							
BP							
RP							
W							
TIME							
	HRS. MINS.	HRS. MINS.	HRS. MINS.	HRS. MINS.	HRS. MINS.	HRS. MINS.	HRS. MINS.

	SUN	MON	TUES	WED	THUR	FRI	SAT
CR							
BP							
RP							
W							
TIME							
	HRS. MINS.	HRS. MINS.	HRS. MINS.	HRS. MINS.	HRS. MINS.	HRS. MINS.	HRS. MINS.

RECAPITULATION FOR MONTH: TOTAL TIME: _____ HRS. _____ MINS.

WEIGHT AT BEGINNING OF MONTH: WEIGHT AT END OF MONTH:

CR=CARDIAC RECOVER BP=BLOOD PRESSURE RP=RESTING PULSE W=WEIGHT

MONTH: (FILL IN DATES)

	SUN	MON	TUES	WED	THUR	FRI	SAT
CR							
BP							
RP							
W							
TIME							
	HRS. MINS.	HRS. MINS.	HRS. MINS.	HRS. MINS.	HRS. MINS.	HRS. MINS.	HRS. MINS.

	SUN	MON	TUES	WED	THUR	FRI	SAT
CR							
BP							
RP							
W							
TIME							
	HRS. MINS	HRS. MINS.	HRS. MINS.	HRS. MINS.	HRS. MINS.	HRS. MINS.	HRS. MINS.

	SUN	MON	TUES	WED	THUR	FRI	SAT
CR							
BP							
RP							
W							
TIME							
	HRS. MINS.	HRS. MINS.	HRS. MINS.	HRS. MINS.	HRS. MINS.	HRS. MINS.	HRS. MINS.

	SUN	MON	TUES	WED	THUR	FRI	SAT
CR							
BP							
RP							
W							
TIME							
	HRS. MINS.	HRS. MINS.	HRS. MINS.	HRS. MINS.	HRS. MINS.	HRS. MINS.	HRS. MINS.

	SUN	MON	TUES	WED	THUR	FRI	SAT
CR							
BP							
RP							
W							
TIME							
	HRS. MINS.	HRS. MINS.	HRS. MINS.	HRS. MINS.	HRS. MINS.	HRS. MINS.	HRS. MINS.

RECAPITULATION FOR MONTH: TOTAL TIME: _____ HRS. _____ MINS.

WEIGHT AT BEGINNING OF MONTH: WEIGHT AT END OF MONTH:

CR=CARDIAC RECOVER BP=BLOOD PRESSURE RP=RESTING PULSE W=WEIGHT

MONTH: (FILL IN DATES)

	SUN	MON	TUES	WED	THUR	FRI	SAT
CR							
BP							
RP							
W							
TIME							
	HRS. MINS.	HRS. MINS.	HRS. MINS.	HRS. MINS.	HRS. MINS.	HRS. MINS.	HRS. MINS.

	SUN	MON	TUES	WED	THUR	FRI	SAT
CR							
BP							
RP							
W							
TIME							
	HRS. MINS	HRS. MINS.	HRS. MINS.	HRS. MINS.	HRS. MINS.	HRS. MINS.	HRS. MINS.

	SUN	MON	TUES	WED	THUR	FRI	SAT
CR							
BP							
RP							
W							
TIME							
	HRS. MINS.	HRS. MINS.	HRS. MINS.	HRS. MINS.	HRS. MINS.	HRS. MINS.	HRS. MINS.

	SUN	MON	TUES	WED	THUR	FRI	SAT
CR							
BP							
RP							
W							
TIME							
	HRS. MINS.	HRS. MINS.	HRS. MINS.	HRS. MINS.	HRS. MINS.	HRS. MINS.	HRS. MINS.

	SUN	MON	TUES	WED	THUR	FRI	SAT
CR							
BP							
RP							
W							
TIME							
	HRS. MINS.	HRS. MINS.	HRS. MINS.	HRS. MINS.	HRS. MINS.	HRS. MINS.	HRS. MINS

RECAPITULATION FOR MONTH: TOTAL TIME: ______ HRS. ______ MINS.

WEIGHT AT BEGINNING OF MONTH: WEIGHT AT END OF MONTH:

CR=CARDIAC RECOVER BP=BLOOD PRESSURE RP=RESTING PULSE W=WEIGH

MONTH: (FILL IN DATES)

	SUN	MON	TUES	WED	THUR	FRI	SAT
CR							
BP							
RP							
W							
TIME							
	HRS. MINS.	HRS. MINS.	HRS. MINS.	HRS. MINS.	HRS. MINS.	HRS. MINS.	HRS. MINS.

	SUN	MON	TUES	WED	THUR	FRI	SAT
CR							
BP							
RP							
W							
TIME							
	HRS. MINS.	HRS. MINS.	HRS. MINS.	HRS. MINS.	HRS. MINS.	HRS. MINS.	HRS. MINS.

	SUN	MON	TUES	WED	THUR	FRI	SAT
CR							
BP							
RP							
W							
TIME							
	HRS. MINS.	HRS. MINS.	HRS. MINS.	HRS. MINS.	HRS. MINS.	HRS. MINS.	HRS. MINS.

	SUN	MON	TUES	WED	THUR	FRI	SAT
CR							
BP							
RP							
W							
TIME							
	HRS. MINS.	HRS. MINS.	HRS. MINS.	HRS. MINS.	HRS. MINS.	HRS. MINS.	HRS. MINS.

	SUN	MON	TUES	WED	THUR	FRI	SAT
CR							
BP							
RP							
W							
TIME							
	HRS. MINS.	HRS. MINS.	HRS. MINS.	HRS. MINS.	HRS. MINS.	HRS. MINS.	HRS. MINS.

RECAPITULATION FOR MONTH: TOTAL TIME: ______ HRS. ______ MINS.

WEIGHT AT BEGINNING OF MONTH: WEIGHT AT END OF MONTH:

CR=CARDIAC RECOVER BP=BLOOD PRESSURE RP=RESTING PULSE W=WEIGHT

MONTH: (FILL IN DATES)

	SUN	MON	TUES	WED	THUR	FRI	SAT
CR							
BP							
RP							
W							
TIME							
	HRS. MINS.	HRS. MINS.	HRS. MINS.	HRS. MINS.	HRS. MINS.	HRS. MINS.	HRS. MINS.

	SUN	MON	TUES	WED	THUR	FRI	SAT
CR							
BP							
RP							
W							
TIME							
	HRS. MINS.	HRS. MINS.	HRS. MINS.	HRS. MINS.	HRS. MINS.	HRS. MINS.	HRS. MINS.

	SUN	MON	TUES	WED	THUR	FRI	SAT
CR							
BP							
RP							
W							
TIME							
	HRS. MINS.	HRS. MINS.	HRS. MINS.	HRS. MINS.	HRS. MINS.	HRS. MINS.	HRS. MINS.

	SUN	MON	TUES	WED	THUR	FRI	SAT
CR							
BP							
RP							
W							
TIME							
	HRS. MINS.	HRS. MINS.	HRS. MINS.	HRS. MINS.	HRS. MINS.	HRS. MINS.	HRS. MINS.

	SUN	MON	TUES	WED	THUR	FRI	SAT
CR							
BP							
RP							
W							
TIME							
	HRS. MINS.	HRS. MINS.	HRS. MINS.	HRS. MINS.	HRS. MINS.	HRS. MINS.	HRS. MINS.

RECAPITULATION FOR MONTH: TOTAL TIME: ______ HRS. ______ MINS.

WEIGHT AT BEGINNING OF MONTH: WEIGHT AT END OF MONTH:

CR=CARDIAC RECOVER BP=BLOOD PRESSURE RP=RESTING PULSE W=WEIGHT

MONTH: (FILL IN DATES)

	SUN	MON	TUES	WED	THUR	FRI	SAT
CR							
BP							
RP							
W							
TIME							
	HRS. MINS.	HRS. MINS.	HRS. MINS.	HRS. MINS.	HRS. MINS.	HRS. MINS.	HRS. MINS.

	SUN	MON	TUES	WED	THUR	FRI	SAT
CR							
BP							
RP							
W							
TIME							
	HRS. MINS.	HRS. MINS.	HRS. MINS.	HRS. MINS.	HRS. MINS.	HRS. MINS.	HRS. MINS.

	SUN	MON	TUES	WED	THUR	FRI	SAT
CR							
BP							
RP							
W							
TIME							
	HRS. MINS.	HRS. MINS.	HRS. MINS.	HRS. MINS.	HRS. MINS.	HRS. MINS.	HRS. MINS.

	SUN	MON	TUES	WED	THUR	FRI	SAT
CR							
BP							
RP							
W							
TIME							
	HRS. MINS.	HRS. MINS.	HRS. MINS.	HRS. MINS.	HRS. MINS.	HRS. MINS.	HRS. MINS.

	SUN	MON	TUES	WED	THUR	FRI	SAT
CR							
BP							
RP							
W							
TIME							
	HRS. MINS.	HRS. MINS.	HRS. MINS.	HRS. MINS.	HRS. MINS.	HRS. MINS.	HRS. MINS.

RECAPITULATION FOR MONTH: TOTAL TIME: ______ HRS. ______ MINS.

WEIGHT AT BEGINNING OF MONTH: WEIGHT AT END OF MONTH:

CR=CARDIAC RECOVER BP=BLOOD PRESSURE RP=RESTING PULSE W=WEIGHT

MONTH: (FILL IN DATES)

	SUN	MON	TUES	WED	THUR	FRI	SAT
CR							
BP							
RP							
W							
TIME							
	HRS. MINS.	HRS. MINS.	HRS. MINS.	HRS. MINS.	HRS. MINS.	HRS. MINS.	HRS. MINS.

	SUN	MON	TUES	WED	THUR	FRI	SAT
CR							
BP							
RP							
W							
TIME							
	HRS. MINS	HRS. MINS.	HRS. MINS.	HRS. MINS.	HRS. MINS.	HRS. MINS.	HRS. MINS.

	SUN	MON	TUES	WED	THUR	FRI	SAT
CR							
BP							
RP							
W							
TIME							
	HRS. MINS.	HRS. MINS.	HRS. MINS.	HRS. MINS.	HRS. MINS.	HRS. MINS.	HRS. MINS.

	SUN	MON	TUES	WED	THUR	FRI	SAT
CR							
BP							
RP							
W							
TIME							
	HRS. MINS.	HRS. MINS.	HRS. MINS.	HRS. MINS.	HRS. MINS.	HRS. MINS.	HRS. MINS.

	SUN	MON	TUES	WED	THUR	FRI	SAT
CR							
BP							
RP							
W							
TIME							
	HRS. MINS.	HRS. MINS.	HRS. MINS.	HRS. MINS.	HRS. MINS.	HRS. MINS.	HRS. MINS.

RECAPITULATION FOR MONTH: TOTAL TIME: ______ HRS. ______ MINS.

WEIGHT AT BEGINNING OF MONTH: WEIGHT AT END OF MONTH:

CR=CARDIAC RECOVER BP=BLOOD PRESSURE RP=RESTING PULSE W=WEIGHT

CHAPTER 12

The Walking Exercises

Picture yourself in motion, walking, and visualize the effect on your body. It should immediately become apparent to you that your leg muscles receive great exercise from the activity. But what about the rest of your body—your stomach, back, and chest; your arms, shoulders, and neck? What does walking do for these generally underexercised areas? Come to think of it, does walking do anything for them at all?

Admittedly, walking does concentrate on the legs and hips, with only limited muscular involvement above the waist. Accordingly, the legs are particularly well-exercised, for just about every leg muscle is somehow involved in the stretching, pulling, and swinging that is required for walking movement. While other forms of lower limb activity emphasize only certain groups of muscles (running, for example, concentrates on the calves and the quadriceps), walking calls them all into play and promotes natural, even contours and overall firmness. Since over 50 percent of our entire muscular mass is located below the waist, walking enhances the strength and firmness of the majority of our muscles all at once, in a relatively short period of time. While this is good, it's not good enough. For a firm body from head to toe, something else is definitely needed.

With the help of Elizabeth Spedale, a physical therapist, I have developed a series of exercises that can be implemented while you walk. The purpose here is threefold.

1. Get the aerobic exercise you need in the safest way possible—walking.
2. Develop all the muscles of your body, not merely the leg muscles.
3. Add diversity to your walks, thus providing ongoing relief from the boredom that accompanies any routine form of exercise.

This should be your approach:

Before beginning the walking exercises, stand undressed in front of a full-length mirror and evaluate your body. Starting with your face and working down to your feet, determine what areas need the most work; where you are the weakest, what parts of your body need to be strengthened, slimmed, or built up. Take notes.

From this chapter, select the proper exercises for your particular problem. Then, once you feel familiar with the basic core of the program—the strolling warm-up, the 12 consecutive aerobic minutes and the slow-walking cooling-off period—you can add the walking exercises to improve the condition of specific parts of your body. The exercises are, of course, totally optional and should be performed *only* during the warm-up and cooling-off periods, before and after the important 12 minutes of nonstop aerobic walking.

Physiologically, it is best to perform upper body exercises during the warm-up because they will help raise your heart rate to the proper aerobic target zone. Lower limb exercises should be performed during the cooling-off period, after the aerobic 12 minutes. In this way, the blood that has accumulated in the muscles of your legs and hips can be effectively pumped back into your central circulation. Please follow this procedure to derive the maximum benefit from the walking program in the most effective manner possible.

Here are the different muscle groups and how to exercise them while you walk.

Muscles of the face

The facial muscles are used for mastication (biting and chewing) and expression. While the *masticators* get moderate exercise every day when you eat, the muscles of facial expression do not. Consequently, fat accumulates in the face, and slowly but surely, you develop a saggy, droopy appearance. To slow down and reverse this process, employ the facial exercises I will now describe. You may get some stares from your fellow pedestrians, but don't let that bother you. In time they will be staring at your great, new, healthy body.

Located on the forehead, the *frontalis* is the muscle that raises the eyebrows and wrinkles the forehead. Put this muscle to work right now in order to appreciate its action. Remember the movement and perform it 50 times during your warm-up if you want to enhance its action. You don't have to do it during every warm-up, but you might spend one week working on the muscles of your face and neck, the next week working on your arms and shoulders, the third week on your chest and abdomen, and so on, until you have covered your entire body. Then start them all over again.

And remember, all muscles burn up calories, so even the simple repeated flexion of the frontalis, combined with the other walking exercises, will aid in the fabulous slimming effect of the walking program.

Next, there's the *platysma,* a large sheet-like muscle that covers the front of the neck, running from the collarbone to the lower lip. By flexing it, you will pull the lower lip and the corners of the mouth downward, the neck will slightly widen, and the collarbone will rise. Try it and overly accentuate its action. In so doing, you should feel the muscle move throughout your neck and chin. The flexing action of the platysma is great to tighten the neck and lower face, thus removing the double chin that often develops here. During your warm-up, repeat this action as many times as you can in an attempt to fatigue the muscle. For most people, 50 contractions is sufficient.

The cheek muscles, those that are used for blowing, are called the *buccinators,* and the multi-layered muscle that exercises the mouth is called the *obicularis oris.* By filling the cheeks with air, protruding the lips, and slowly blowing the air out of the mouth, both of these muscle groups are drawn into action. The lip muscles can be exercised by closing the mouth and tightly pressing the lips together. Hold this position, then protrude the lips as far as they will go. Finally, press them back against your teeth. Try it a few times right now. If repeated over and over, you will find that these exercises not only strengthen the facial muscles and uplift the face, they also help to keep the teeth in proper alignment—an added benefit.

In first attempting the walking exercises, especially those of the face, it is a good idea to practice them in front of a mirror until you have learned proper movements. Once you have mastered each individual action, you are then ready to incorporate these exercises into the overall walking program. Spend one solid week on facial exercises, and perform them, as I have mentioned, during your walking warm-ups—for the eight minutes or so that it takes to raise your heartbeat to the proper exercise level. Each individual muscle group should be exercised until it is fatigued, about 50 flexions.

Muscles of the arms and shoulder

Most laborious tasks and household chores require strenuous use of the arm and shoulder muscles. If these areas are allowed to weaken with age, the ability to perform normal daily jobs is greatly compromised. In addition, the overall contour of the body will suffer.

The muscles of the arms and shoulders tend to be huge in comparison to the other muscles of the body. One of the largest muscles of this group is the *pectoralis.* This muscle is located on the front of the chest and extends from the collarbone to the rib cage, just under the nipple. In women, it lies directly beneath the breast.

Since the pectoralis also has an attachment on the arm, near the shoulder joint, it serves to raise the arms and draw them across the front of the chest to the opposite side of the body.

Another large muscle located at the shoulder is the *deltoid.* It runs from the very top of the arm to midway between the shoulder and the elbow. When contracted, it lifts the arm up and away from the side of the body, a movement called abduction. This action is opposed by two other large muscles, the *latissimus dorsi* and the *teres major,* both of which arise on the back and attach to the arm near the shoulder joint. When these are activated, they pull the extended arm back to the side, an action called adduction.

With intentional arm movement, back and forth, up and down, the major muscles of the shoulder, both the abductors and adductors can be exercised as you walk. One of the simplest methods is to perform fully-extended arm circles, first with the right arm, then with the left, ten times each, forward and backward. Or you can raise your arms to shoulder level and hold this position for one full minute. In this case, however, both arms should be raised together in order to maintain proper balance through the exercise.

You will also find that arm raises require the participation of the *trapezius,* a large triangular muscle that runs down the spine from the neck to the mid-back and also attaches at the shoulder. By shrugging the shoulders, trying to make them touch your ears, you significantly work the trapezius and strengthen its action. Try it. Pull your shoulders back, then as high as they will go. Now, depress them, forcing them as low as you can. Up and down, up and down, as many times as you are able, 50 if possible. With each procedure, you should literally feel the trapezius at work, and form a mental picture of its action and location.

Finally, to enlist the participation of all the muscles at the shoulder, vertical arm swings can be employed. Moving the arms in unison, swing them as high over your head as they will go, feeling the stretch throughout your torso. As they swing back down, bend slightly at the waist to add to the momentum. Twenty repetitions is fine for this particular exercise.

For a variation of the vertical method, swing your arms horizontally in front of your chest so that they cross in the midline. When you swing them back as far as they will go, expand the chest with a large breath of air. Do this exercise with the elbows straight, and bent, for maximum benefit. Ten times each way. The arms should always be at shoulder height.

Forearm and hand

These exercises will not only strengthen the hand, but will also increase the power of the lower arm. As you perform them, you should feel the various muscle groups tighten and relax in response to your efforts.

The muscles of the forearm and hand, too numerous to mention here, can be exercised simply by opening and closing the hand. When the hand is open, an attempt should be made to stretch the fingers and separate them as much as possible. When the hand is closed, a tight fist should be held for five seconds. These exercises should be repeated 20 times each. An alternative is to carry a small rubber ball with you when you walk. By firmly squeezing the ball 50 times with each hand, the same results will be realized—the hand and forearm will be strengthened.

Likewise, the wrist should be flexed (bent forward) and held for five seconds, then extended (bent backward) and held for five seconds, twenty-five times each way.

The abdomen

Now that we have focused on the face, neck, shoulders, arms, chest, and back, we are ready to move to a very important area, the abdomen. Of all the sections of the body, it is probably the most neglected in terms of exercise. In my program, the abdominal muscles will be strengthened along with the diaphragm, utilizing the deep-breathing exercise that I described in the breathing chapter.

To reiterate briefly, as you breathe in deeply, the *diaphragm,* and internal flap-like muscle that separates the chest from the abdomen, contracts downward and enlarges the chest cavity. A vacuum is thus created in the chest, and air is drawn into the lungs. With exercise, the body's demand for air and oxygen greatly increases, so this breathing exercise will not only help fill that demand, it will also strengthen the diaphragm and abdominal muscles. Here is how to do it.

As you walk, breath in very deeply and concentrate on forcing your stomach muscles out at the same time. Expand your chest and raise your clavicles as explained in the breathing chapter. Air will rush into your lungs, filling even the lower lobes that normally remain contracted with shallow breathing. Hold the breath five seconds. As you exhale, force all the air out of your lungs and concentrate on pulling your stomach way in. Hold this position for five seconds, then repeat the procedure 20 times. If you become light-headed, breathe slower and walk faster.

As previously mentioned, all the above exercises should be performed only during the warm-up period before you enter the aerobic segment. The following exercises should be done through the cooling off.

Hips and legs

The major muscles of the hip include the *gluteus maximus* and *gluteus medius*. The largest of these is the gluteus maximus, which comprises the buttocks and pulls the thighs directly backward. The gluteus medius lies at the side of the hip and draws the legs apart into a split position. Both of these muscles give your hips their size and shape.

While the gluteus maximus is well exercised by walking, it can further be strengthened by consciously intensifying its action. When you walk, place your right hand over your right buttock. Now, as your leg goes back with each step you take, tense the gluteus in excess of what is required for normal functioning. You should feel the muscle harden under your hand. As you continue to walk, alternatively tense the right, then the left buttock. With practice, you will no longer need to feel the muscular contraction with your hand. You will know how to perform the exercise and do it without manual assistance.

Moving down the leg from the hip, the next group of muscles we encounter are the thigh muscles. These comprise two major groups: the *quadriceps* at the front of the thigh, and the *hamstrings* at the back of the thigh. While the front group, the "quads," are responsible for bending the leg at the hip and straightening the lower leg at the knee, the rear group, the hamstrings, are needed to flex the lower leg at the knee. Thus, the action of these two muscle groups oppose each other.

To exercise these opposite groups specifically, knee raises are helpful. As you walk, instead of swinging your legs well in front of your body with each step, bring your knees up to the level of your waist. The flexing action at the hip and the bending of the knee will require the participation of both the front and back thigh muscle. You should feel both groups tense with each exercise, and as the muscles contract, they squeeze the blood that has collected in them during your walking back into the central circulation. Fifty knee raises is sufficient.

Lower leg

Heel raises and toe walking can be used to specifically exercise the muscles of your lower leg. During your walks, the first contact with the ground is made by your heel. Right after the heel strikes, weight is shifted to the ball and toes of your foot, and the heel is lifted off the ground. In order to exercise the front muscles of the lower leg, simply keep the foot firmly flexed throughout all phases of your gait and walk only on your heel. Vice versa, to exercise the calf muscles, walk on your toes to accentuate the heel-raising phase of your gait. Both of these exercises should be performed for approximately one minute each. But remember, they should only be done as part of the walking exercises and are not meant to be done during the aerobic portion of your walk when normal gait is imperative.

By doing the walking exercises before and after the aerobic section of my walking program, you can strengthen all of the muscles in your entire body, not just the muscles below your waist. Overall body strength can be much improved, and a more fit appearance will result. But, as I said at the beginning of this chapter, these exercises are totally optional. They are for your particular needs and should be performed selectively to improve special parts of your body—your most troublesome areas. If you perform them regularly, you will certainly be rewarded.

CHAPTER 13

Dressing to Walk

Of all the advantages to walking, possibly the most obvious is the walking wardrobe. Unlike all other sports or exercises, walking can be done in casual every day clothing . . . no matter what you have on, you're always ready for a walk. Of course, there are some outfits and footwear that are superior to others. And some apparel should be avoided whenever possible. But, generally, any of your clothing will make an acceptable walking outfit. To highlight the most appropriate walking wardrobe, let's now take a look at the kinds of clothing that are best and consider the various circumstances that require special consideration. We'll start from the ground up.

Shoes

While some primitive cultures still go barefoot today, the overall need for shoes was established a long time ago. No doubt, our ancient ancestors found protection from the cold and the damp, the rocks and the brush, by wrapping their feet in animal skins or strapping sandals to their soles. From those early beginnings to the present time, shoes have taken on a multiplicity of shapes and forms to accommodate a variety of terrains and suit a host of different needs.

For the rice paddies of Asia and the tulip farms of Holland, a wooden shoe emerged. Where the women of wealth and taste aspired to the heights of fashion, high heels carried them there. And just a few short years ago, the high toe, negative heel made its presence known and its manufacturers rich. Yet, with all the different styles and shapes that have come and gone, the basic walking shoe still remains. Its character is basic and sensible; a low wide heel, a broad toe, and a secure fit. But other points are wisely considered.

For instance, to insure comfort, the foot should have ample room to move and breathe, but the heel should not ride up and down in the shoe. Lacing should secure the fit and support the arch without cutting into the foot. Heels and soles should be made of nonskid material. And, to prevent sticks, stones, sand, and dirt from entering the shoe through the laces and eyelets, a broad tongue should be present. (You will also find that a thick broad tongue prevents chafing at the top of the foot.) Finally, a cushioned inner sole will make the going much easier by absorbing the shock that occurs each time the foot meets the ground. Since few shoes come with an adequately cushioned insole, I strongly suggest that you purchase a pair of foam rubber inserts and place them in your favorite walking shoes. They make a world of difference.

Even stylish shoes with a moderate heel can be worn in comfort if they are well made and well fitted. With the addition of a foot pad or a toe cushion, just about any shoe can be customized to meet individual needs.

When special walks are planned, further considerations must be entertained. Hikers will want the added support and protection that can only be provided by a half boot, one that ties about the ankle. These will prevent many strains and sprains. Waterproofing is also desirable unless the hiker intends to slosh his way back to civilization.

Socks

For daily half-hour walks and for the trip to and from the office, one pair of ordinary socks is sufficient. (Cotton socks are probably best since they are absorbent and nonallergenic.) However, for the longer weekend walks and for extended hikes, two pairs of socks are recommended. The inner socks, which should be thin and well fitted, will reduce the friction between your shoes and your feet and prevent painful blisters. The outer socks, thicker and more absorbent, will soak up perspiration, insulate, and reduce pavement pounding, thus saving your shoes as well as your feet.

When purchasing your socks, stick with silks, wools, or cottons and avoid synthetic materials for they are not absorbent and they tend to ride and bind. Plus, beware of socks with broad seams and thick overstitching. These will probably irritate your feet if they are worn on long outings as the seams will press into your skin and cause an inflammation.

You women who wear hose and fashion shoes during the day have your own special problems. On hot days your feet will sweat, and your nylons can't absorb the moisture. On cold days your feet will freeze because the hose provide little insulation. Then, too, stockings tend to bind. For you, the alternatives are few but I do have some suggestions. Some stocking manufacturers are aware of your problems and make hose with cotton inserts. These prevent bunching at the toes and will make your walks more enjoyable. However, as an overall solution to your stocking dilemma, they are inadequate. So here's a better answer. Keep a pair of fashion shoes at work and wear boots or walking shoes to and from the office. You can wear socks over your stockings for warmth and absorption and no one will ever know. Then, when you get to work, peel the boots and socks and step into a more fashionable shoe. At lunch time or when it's time to go home, don the socks and the walking shoes once again and go on your merry way. Your feet will love you for it.

Finally, an absorbent powder will help keep your feet dry and comfortable throughout the day. It will also help prevent blisters.

Clothing

Finding an appropriate walking outfit is a relatively simple task. For myself and just about every other man, a walking outfit constitutes the clothes of the day. Regardless of whether we wear a pair of shorts and a golf shirt or a tuxedo complete with tails, we're ready to go for a walk. Women, on the other hand, cannot be quite so extemporaneous. At times, fashion makes things more difficult for them. And many a woman has had to decline the pleasures of a moonlit stroll because of a long evening gown or a tight skirt. But times are changing and fashion is what you make it, so a woman with a mind to walk can adjust her wardrobe accordingly. A narrow skirt can be tailor-made for walking with the addition of a long side slit. Not only will this make the skirt more functional, it will also make it a bit sexier. Pants and pant suits are readily available in department stores around the country.

As you become more involved with your walking, you will ultimately discover that weather dictates what clothes must be worn.

On warm days it pays to wear clothes of light colors and light fabrics. Naturally, the reverse applies in colder weather. But what happens when the weather is unpredictable and a long walk is planned? In New England they have a saying: "If you don't like the weather, just stick around a few minutes . . . it's bound to change." So, like a prudent New Englander, you must always be prepared. Here are some suggestions:

Wear several layers of relatively light clothing. The outer garments can always be removed and tied about the waist or thrown over the shoulder if you become too warm. But if the sun ducks behind a cloud and you begin to cool off, you will at least have something to put back on. Then, too, a multi-layered outfit will provide excellent insulation in both the summer and the winter. In hot weather, wear cool cotton underclothing and a light weight cotton shirt. When it gets colder, add a colorful wool sweater. As winter approaches, thermal underwear coupled with a wool shirt, a sweater, and a coat or jacket will serve you well. The important thing to remember is that layering is insulation that can be added or removed at a moment's notice, giving you an edge over the weather.

And don't get caught in the rain.

As many avid walkers will testify, a wet walk can be just as pleasant as a walk in the sun . . . if you are appropriately dressed. So add a smart raincoat to your wardrobe, and also a pair of boots or rubbers. Then, be sure to put them to good use, for the solitude and beauty of a rainy walk should be known to everyone.

Here's a helpful tip: you might also buy an inexpensive, lightweight, foldup raincoat or rainsuit that can be carried in your pocket or purse for unpredictable outings. I personally have both, the coat and the suit, and find them indispensable. Folding into a package about the size of a pocket camera, they can be placed in the car's glove box or in a desk drawer at work. In a pinch, they're great and they cost less than five dollars.

Hats

In Russia, the esteem of a man is reflected in the quality of his hat. Elite professionals, holding high positions in government and industry, want expensive hats of fine quality. Less prominent workers sport rugged, durable hats that are designed for warmth and longevity. Those men who wear no hats at all are viewed askance.

Here in America, things are different. Persuaded by fashion rather than practicality, Americans have long abandoned their hats in favor of curly locks and elaborate coiffures. In the snow and the rain or under the blazing sun, Americans prefer to go bareheaded rather than don a hat for comfort and protection. But this attitude is ridiculous. You see, hats are very important articles of clothing. They protect the head, face, and neck from sunburn on bright, sunny days and, in so doing prevent the aging effect the sun has on the skin. In addition, they shade the eyes and reduce glare, thereby aiding vision and preventing the headaches that come from a day of squinting.

By covering the head in winter, a hat will aid in warming the entire body, and will reduce the overall amount of clothing you need to stay warm. Why? Because the scalp is a major site of heat loss, like your hands, arms, legs, and feet. When your head is uncovered on a cold day, the blood flowing through your scalp loses its warmth and returns to the heart a little bit cooler. Consequently, the temperature of your whole body is reduced. Wearing a hat prevents this generalized cooling effect by insulating the scalp and preserving the blood's warmth.

By dressing appropriately and anticipating any change in the weather, you will undoubtedly find greater enjoyment in your walks. Undaunted by the cold and the rain, unimpeded by blisters, you can walk anywhere you choose, anytime, in any season. More importantly, by having the correct clothes for walking, you can take advantage of all walking opportunities, wherever they arise.

Walk in style
Walk in grace
But above all, walk.
You'll feel great.

And remember, you're only as pretty as you feel.

One final reminder. Whenever you spend time outdoors, use a good sunscreen on your face and lips for protection from the elements. Sunscreens are the most effective agents you can buy to prevent skin cancer and the aging effects that are caused by sunlight.

CHAPTER 14

Walking and Calories

It's no secret that walking burns calories, but does it burn enough to be effective as a dietary aid? For an accurate appraisal of the situation, let's examine the mathematics of calorie consumption and weight loss. After all, from a purely objective standpoint, numbers tell the whole story.

For example, each pound of fat in our body stores 3,500 calories of energy. When we fail to eat enough food to meet our daily energy requirements, we must draw on this fat for fuel, releasing the calories it contains. When an extra 3,500 calories is needed, for instance, we would have to burn away one pound of fat and we would lose one pound of body weight. Vice versa, if we eat 3,500 calories *more* than we need we would store an additional pound of fat and we would gain an additional pound of body weight. Regardless of whether it takes a day, a week, a month, or a year, 3,500 calories equals one pound of fat, gained or lost. Now the question arises: how many calories do we burn when we walk? And, is the caloric consumption of walking sufficient to produce a noticeable weight loss? Since the answers to these questions depend on walking speed and distance, I refer you to the following ACTIVITY CALORIE CHART.

ACTIVITY CALORIE CHART

ACTIVITY	CALORIE EXPENDITURE cals/minute	COMMENT
Strolling	2.0-2.5	No aerobic effects.
Horseshoe Toss	3.0-4.0	Moderate exercise for shoulders and arms.
Bowling	3.5-4.5	Same as horseshoes.
Fishing	3.0-4.0	Fresh air and relaxation are major benefits here.
Golf with power cart	3.0-4.0	Moderate exercise for upper body. No aerobic effects however.
Shuffleboard	3.0-4.0	Same as horseshoes.
Table Tennis	3.5-6.0	Develops quick reflexes and good eye-hand coordination.
Archery	3.5-5.0	Arm and chest strength enhanced.
Hunting	3.5-5.0	Mild aerobic benefit.
Dancing	4.0-7.0	If prolonged, mild aerobic effect.
Hiking/Walking 3 mph	4.0-7.0	Adequate dynamic exercise for deconditioned people.
Cycling 8 mph	5.0-7.0	Same as Hiking/Walking.
Golf, carrying clubs	5.0-7.0	Provides aerobic benefit if exercise heart rate is achieved and sustained.

Tennis, doubles	5.0-7.0	Same as Golfing carrying clubs.
Calisthenics	5.0-7.0	Promotes muscular strength.
Canoeing/Rowing	5.0-7.0	Good aerobic effect if prolonged and continuous.
Softball	3.5-5.0	Eye-hand coordination enhanced but activity is too intermittent for aerobic effect.
Volleyball	3.5-6.0	Activity is too intermittent for aerobic benefit.
Sledding	4.0-6.0	Good overall exertion but limited aerobic benefit.
Tennis, singles	6.0-8.0	Aerobic effect realized if player moves about continuously for 30 mins.
Scuba diving	6.0-8.0	Good aerobic effect if swimming is continuous.
Cycling 12 mph	7.0-8.0	Positive aerobic effect. Fitness enhanced.
Snow skiing	7.0-8.0	Predominantly isometric. Activity is too short.
Water skiing	7.0-8.0	Hazardous for cardiacs.
Jogging 5 mph	7.0-8.0	Dynamic aerobic exercise.
WALKING 5 mph	7.0-8.0	Same as above.
Swimming	7.0-8.0	Same as above.
Handball	7.0-8.0	Activity is strenuous but not sufficiently continuous for positive aerobic effect. May be hazardous for cardiacs.
Racquetball	7.0-8.0	Same as above.
Squash	7.0-8.0	Same as above.

Snowshoeing	8.0-10.0	Dynamic aerobic exercise, great conditioner. Too strenuous for the unfit or those with pre-existing cardiac problems.
Cross-country skiing	8.0-10.0	Same as Snowshoeing
Running 5 mph	10.0-11.0	Dynamic aerobic exercise, great conditioner. Too strenuous for the unfit or those with pre-existing heart disease.
Cycling 13 mph	10.00-11.0	Dynamic aerobic exercise, great conditioner. Too strenuous for the unfit or those with pre-existing medical problems.
Competitive Squash, Handball, Racquetball	10.0-11.0	Rigorous competition in these strenuous sports provides great exercise, but they should only be performed by those in tiptop condition. They are very dangerous for anyone out of shape or in questionable health.
Running 6 mph 7 mph 8 mph	11.00+	Dynamic aerobic exercise, great conditioner. Only for the athlete or those in excellent physical condition.

As you can see from the chart, the faster you walk, the more calories you burn. A simple stroll of one to two miles per hour, or the casual stop-and-go walking that characterizes our daily movement requires only 150 calories per hour. At this speed, which is far below the rate needed to raise your pulse to the now familiar 75 percent maximum level, it would take almost a full day (23½ hours) of continuous strolling to burn the 3,500 calories needed to lose that one pound of fat. Furthermore, no aerobic benefit would be derived at this minimal level of exertion.

On the other hand, walking at a faster pace, say four to five miles per hour, provides all of the aerobic benefits that you expect from exercise and also burns about 450 calories per hour. Now, instead of 23½ hours, only seven and one-half hours are needed to burn off one pound of fat. That's the equivalent of two pounds per month, 24 pounds per year, if you walk only 30 minutes each day. And while this might not seem like much of a loss, it is quite significant, for it resembles the way we gain weight: a little at a time, a couple pounds per month.

Also remember, these figures reveal the weight loss that results solely from walking and do not take any self-imposed dietary restrictions into consideration. They indicate a two pound weight loss each month if your walk just 30 minutes each day and never attempt to diet.

Interestingly, walking is safer and more effective than dieting alone in causing beneficial weight reduction. As you gain weight from overeating and underexercising, fat is deposited throughout your body—around your internal organs, between muscle fibers, and under your skin. While dieting is quick to remove the superficial skin fat, it is slow to remove the deeper fat, especially those deposits that are buried between skeletal muscle fibers. In order to get rid of these hidden fatty reserves, some people resort to starvation diets or fad diets that are nutritionally dangerous. This extreme type of dieting has many harmful effects. Since essential vitamins, minerals, and proteins may be withheld from the body, random muscle wasting and generalized tissue damage can accompany the fat loss. Metabolic imbalances also occur. However, combining walking with a sensible, well-balanced diet, this catastrophe can be avoided. As your energy requirements increase with the physical activity of walking, both the subcutaneous fat and the intramuscular fat are burned away safely. Only in this way does weight loss occur without destruction of muscle. The intramuscular fat fills the energy needs of the surrounding muscles that are hard at work. As these muscles become firmer and stronger with exertion, the internal fat, the marbling, is depleted—the fat is changed to lean.

Because of this change from fat to lean, the increase in caloric consumption that you realize during your walks continues long after the walking ceases. Even while you sleep you will burn more calories because the lean muscle has a much higher *resting* energy requirement and uses up many more calories, minute for minute, than the metabolically inactive fat it replaced.

Your newly exercised muscle is also much more metabolically active than your previous deconditioned muscle. Consequently, sluggish enzyme systems that have been wasted with inactivity become robust, and tiny intracellular energy factories, the mytocondria, become more numerous as the muscle is whipped into shape. The overall effect: greater caloric utilization even in the resting state.

While most adults slowly gain weight as they get older, even though they cut back on their food intake, they rarely understand the cause of their obesity. It's not just food that leads to their overweight, as they suspect; it's their constant physical inactivity. No diet, not even the most stringent, can reduce, reshape, and recondition your body like a good exercise program—like walking.

WALKING AND CALORIES

After years of battling the bulge, the pertinent facts of weight loss are just emerging. The ultimate cure for obesity is exercise. And the best exercise is walking.

So here's what to do if *you* need to lose a few pounds as well as recondition your body.

First, employ the walking program to its fullest extent; walk whenever possible and follow my instructions precisely. At the same time, employ these helpful dietary suggestions:

1. Take a multiple vitamin and mineral supplement every morning. Add to this an extra 1000 mg. of vitamin C and a good B complex vitamin (several small doses through the day are better than one large dose).
2. Have only fruit or fruit juice and coffee or tea for breakfast. Although a hearty breakfast is more nutritious, it is also more caloric.
3. For lunch, have any two of the following four items: soup, salad, fruit, vegetables, as much as you want.
4. At dinner, have any three of the above four items, as much as you want to.
5. Totally avoid fats, oils, sweets, and fried foods.
6. Replace all beverages at lunch and dinner with water. Add fresh lemon for flavor if desired. You may also drink additional water anytime, day or night.
7. As a bonus, you can have six ounces of meat, preferably fish or chicken, four times a week, but no more. The meat should be eaten in place of one soup, salad, fruit or vegetable.

If you follow this diet and walk simultaneously, you can expect to lose about ten pounds the first week, five pounds each week thereafter. But you must walk and diet each day!

CHAPTER 15

Heart Recovery

One of the best ways to determine your overall level of fitness and follow the progress of your exercise is to monitor the beats of your heart. Of all cardiac evaluations, certainly the examination of the physician would be informative, for much can be learned with a stethoscope and a trained ear. Other important, but more elaborate, indicators of cardiac health are electrocardiograms (EKGs, ECGs), both the resting and the stress varieties, plus special laboratory and X-ray studies. However, all these determinations require equipment and assistance which make them impractical for your frequent use. Besides, they would cost you a fortune.

Luckily, there is one valuable test that you can perform yourself. It is called the heart recovery rate and it is an excellent means whereby you can measure your cardiac status on a regular on-going basis, without a doctor, without special equipment. All you need is a wristwatch with a second hand and the following information:

As you already know, whenever you walk, your heart rate temporarily goes up. In fact, for you to be exercising properly, your heart must be pushed to 75 percent of its maximum rate, as we have discussed. But what goes up, must come down. So, at the end of your walk, your heart rate will automatically fall back to its resting level. This decline is absolutely predictable and can be easily measured against time. In addition, its rapidity provides a good indication of the overall fitness of your heart.

Normally, the greatest decline will occur within the first minute after you stop walking. It is this phase of recovery that is vitally important.

After this initial fall, your heart rate will level off for a while, establishing a plateau stage. Since the plateau is variable, lasting from 15 minutes to a couple of hours, it provides little insight into cardiac function and need not be followed.

Finally, after the plateau, a second decline will occur as your heart rate reaches its normal resting level. And, while the resting rate may provide some indication of your cardiac fitness (the lower the better), it is not as informative as the first phase of recovery. Therefore, it is the early recovery that we must emphasize and evaluate, because the faster the initial decline, the stronger your heart.

Since you already know how to take your pulse, you will have no problem measuring your own recovery rate. It's very easy.

Immediately upon completing your walk, before you begin to cool off, take your exercising pulse as you normally would. Count the beats that occur in six seconds and multiply that number by ten. Ideally, you should obtain a rate that is 75 percent of your maximum cardiac output. Next, allow one minute of inactivity to pass and take a second pulse count. This

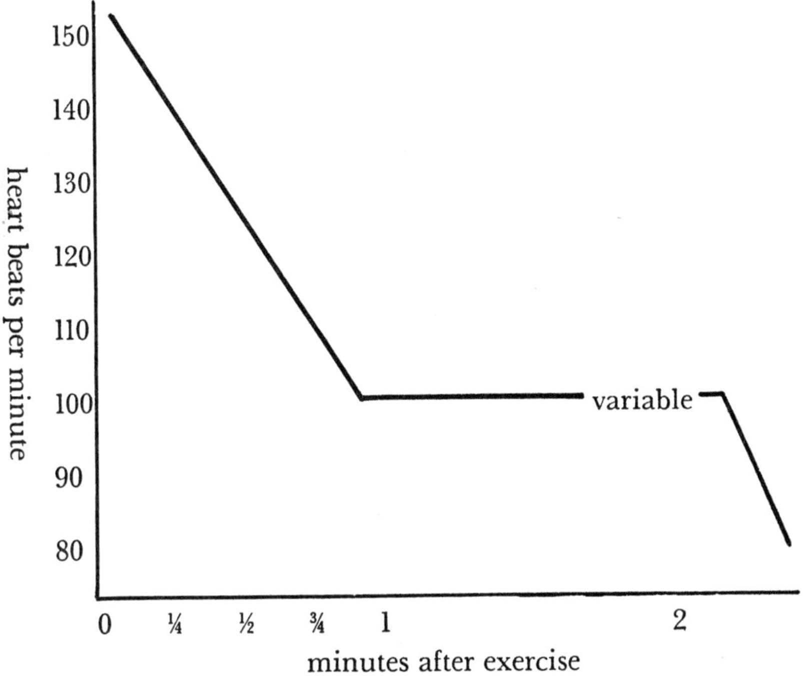

HEART RECOVERY AFTER EXERCISE

time you should notice a significant lowering, since you have already allowed your heart to slow down—*recover*—from the higher exercising level.

Finally, you must subtract the one minute pulse rate from the exercising rate to discover the amount of recovery. Then, divide this difference by ten.

If you end up with a number of two or less, you are in pitiful shape, and your heart is way out of condition. If you get a number between two and three, you are only in fair shape and definitely need more work. A good cardiac status is indicated by a recovery between three and four; however, this can be bettered. People in excellent fitness with strong conditioned hearts will obtain a recovery rate between four and six. And, those in super shape will wind up with a number greater than six.

Where do you stand? What kind of shape are you in? Heart recovery will provide the answers to these questions and dispel your doubt, once and for all.

One final suggestion.

Determine your recovery rate before you begin my walking program so you will have a baseline for future reference. Be sure to write it down in the chart.

After one week of walking, measure your recovery again, and register that number in the chart. Do the same at the end of the second week and the third week and the fourth week and every week thereafter, so you will have an ongoing record. Now, you can make a comparison from week to week, following the progress of your exercise and witnessing for yourself the wonders of walking. You'll be amazed.

CHAPTER 16

Walking after Heart Attack

Of all major illnesses, the heart attack ranks number one in terms of death and debility to middle-aged and elderly Americans. The likelihood of you dying of a heart attack or heart disease is approximately one in three, twice the death rate from cancer, and four times the death rate from stroke.

As I have explained to you in previous chapters, the risk of heart attack can be greatly reduced by following a lifelong exercise program like my walking program. But for many people it is already too late. Millions of Americans have already damaged their hearts and are currently living in the aftermath of a myocardial infarction—a heart attack. Obviously, for them, total prevention is now impossible.

The reasons and causes of a heart attack are well known. With age, the coronary arteries slowly become clogged with fatty cholesterol plaques—a condition known as atherosclerosis—

hardening of the arteries. As the plaque builds up, it slowly reduces the size of the arteries, and blood flow to the heart gradually diminishes.

Adding to the problem and precipitating the actual heart attack, the plaque breaks and a blood clot forms over the partial obstruction, completely closing off the artery to any blood flow. Since the heart muscle beyond the point of obstruction cannot receive the oxygen and nutrients that are carried in the blood, tissue destruction occurs, a heart attack results.

Many people die as a result of their first heart attack, but many others survive. For the survivers, the initial period after the infarction is filled with worry and the fear of death. An acute awareness of the seriousness of their illness occupies their thoughts for weeks or months afterward. And many are so frightened that they restrict their activity totally, literally making themselves invalids. Ironically, the best therapy for these people is physical activity.

Of course, the path back to a normal lifestyle is slow (it must be to prevent further cardiac damage) but with perseverance the cardiac patient can bring himself or herself back to full function. The first step begins in the hospital where the patient again starts to walk. This is followed by progressively increasing activity at home, and ultimately, a return to work in most cases. But how can heart attack victims prevent further damage to their hearts? And how can they improve the quality of their lives?

The answer is simple—they must walk!

By beginning a walking program as soon after the hospitalization as possible, the post heart attack patient begins to realize that all is not lost. Indeed, one of the most important daily activities, moving about, is easy to do. Through graded walking, the fear of sudden death fades, and the patient regains confidence and self-assurance. With each day comes renewed hope in the future.

In the beginning, it is necessary to go slowly. A stroll that elevates the resting pulse ten beats per minute is sufficient. This leisurely pace is readily tolerated for durations of five to ten minutes at a time and can be employed for the first week of walking. Increases of five beats per minute for each week thereafter can then be added to the exercising pulse until 70 percent of the maximum pulse rate for the individual is reached. This is the established norm for cardiac patients and should become their reference standard for aerobic activity.

If mild pain or discomfort is ever experienced during the walks, the pace should be reduced so that the pulse declines slowly and the oxygen requirement for the heart decreases. The discomfort should quickly pass. However, if significant pain arises or persists, an immediate call to the doctor is obviously needed. Other warning signals of possible complications are discussed in Chapter 8 and should always be heeded and respected. Follow-up should be prompt.

By following a strict walking program after a heart attack, there will be both mental and physical rewards for the individual. First and foremost, an interaction with society and the environment will provide a tremendous psychological lift to the heart attack victim. Life begins anew, and hope replaces fear. Second, the heart becomes stronger as new blood vessels slowly bypass the older clogged vessels that initially caused the infarction. This is a lifesaving change because the heart tissues that are literally starving for blood and oxygen become revitalized by the aerobic effects of walking.

Not only will this change help to correct some of the damage that has already been done, it will also reduce the progress of any other blood vessel disease, assuming that the individual becomes diet conscious as well as exercise conscious.

Sometimes, however, when the obstruction of the coronary arteries is so diffuse and severe, it is necessary to replace the damaged arteries with blood vessels taken from elsewhere in the body. This is known as bypass surgery. Again, walking is great therapy following this operation because it will strengthen the heart and promote new blood vessel growth. In addition, the aerobic effects on the body tissues aid healing and encourage rapid recovery from bypass surgery and, in fact, most other forms of cardiac and noncardiac operations.

Naturally, the direction and advice of the attending physician is needed in these cases and his personal sanction is desired. But you can bet that he will be more than willing to help if the heart attack patient is motivated. And what greater motivation is there than life itself?

BEYOND

Not only do you have the knowledge to change your life, you also have the knowledge to change your world.

You can start with your surroundings.

CHAPTER 17

The Vitacourse

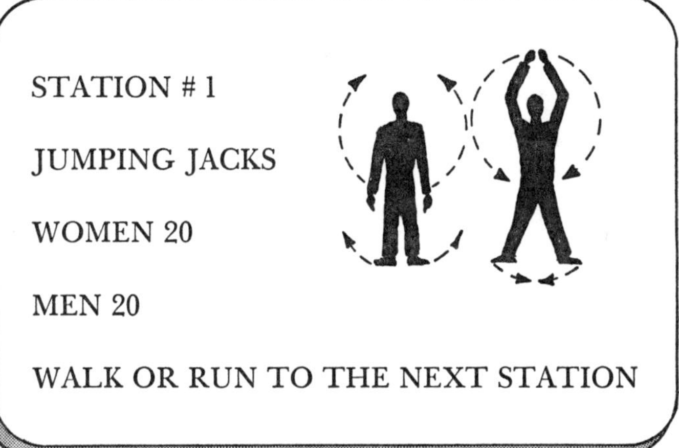

Imagine walking to a local park or playground and finding a sign like the one above. Would you be inclined to follow the instructions? Perhaps you would be curious enough to check out the next station. If you did, you would find a second sign that read:

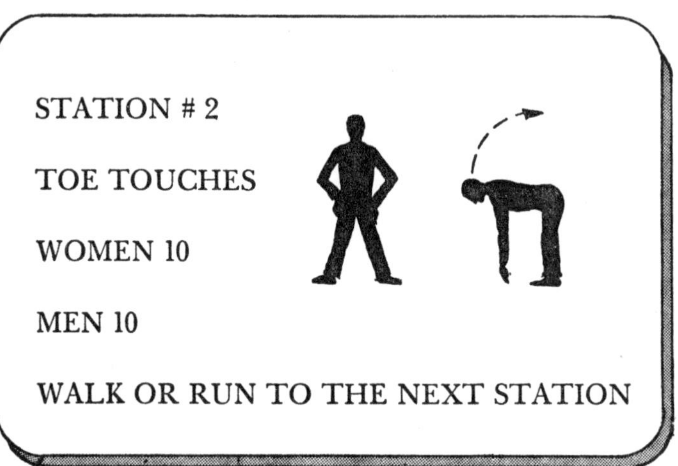

Now what would you do?

Well if you're anything like the hundreds of thousands of other people who have been introduced to the VitaCourse, you would probably continue through all twenty or more exercise stations, performing the activity prescribed, and enjoy the experience enough to return again the following day and every day thereafter.

Developed by the Swiss in the sixties, the VitaCourse is an innovative, self-instructive approach to physical conditioning that combines aerobic exercise with calisthenics and other forms of isotonics. It can be used by people of all ages and all levels of fitness to improve their cardiovascular and respiratory health, increase their strength and flexibility, and enhance their coordination.

The VitaCourse is composed of a series of exercise stations

that are joined together by a walking or jogging trail. At each station, a small sign describes the exercise to be performed, illustrates its movement sequence, and suggests the appropriate number of repetitions for both men and women. While the initial warm-up exercises are simple, the course is so designed as to gradually include more strenuous tasks, then cooling-off exercises at the very end. Special equipment, such as chin-up bars and climbing blocks, are provided where they are needed.

The walking or jogging segments of the course link each station and vary in distance depending on the overall length of the entire course. When the full VitaCourse is one and one-half to two miles long, which is the average, each walking segment is about 100 yards. Consequently, if you walk briskly from one station to the next, perform the required exercise, and quickly move on, you can elevate your pulse and respiratory rates to acceptable aerobic levels. Heart and lung fitness stem from this aerobic activity and complement the muscular strength and coordination that are developed at the isotonic exercise stations. In short, the VitaCourse successfully combines aerobic and nonaerobic exercise in a recreational, self-instructive form.

At the start of the course, an explanatory note, basically similar to the information provided here, prepares you for the experience and also describes certain limitations and precautions for those special participants (cardiacs, etc.) who have a limited capacity to exercise. From the first exercise to the last, you need not worry about overexerting yourself because the course is so skillfully designed that anyone, nine or 90, can handle the activity. But if a particular exercise seems too difficult, forget it and move on to the next station. It's as simple as that.

If there is a VitaCourse near you, I urge you to try it. You need not prepare yourself in any special way; just wear comfortable clothes and a pair of sneakers. Read the initial instructions carefully before beginning the course, then embark on a totally new and exciting exercise adventure. I'm sure you will enjoy it immensely.

If there is not a VitaCourse near you, with a little imagination, you could create a mini one in your own backyard. With the installation of a few simple pieces of apparatus like a chin-up bar and a sit-up bench with individual foot straps, plus an area designated for push-ups, jumping jacks, and deep knee bends, you can literally turn your lawn into an outdoor health spa. Combined with the aerobic benefits of walking and the supplementary walking exercises, all of the health facilities you could ever need would be as close as your own backyard.

For further information about the VitaCourse and the specific exercises stations write: Parscourse, Governor's Council on Physical Fitness, Tallahassee, Florida.

CHAPTER 18

The Perils of Running

Although heart attacks are probably the most dreaded, they constitute only one of the many risks known to runners and joggers. Combined with all the other possible injuries, they cast a forbidding shadow on an otherwise beneficial exercise and frequently place a well-intentioned exerciser in the hospital. These risks seem high, indeed, when compared to the relative safety of walking.

Assuming you survive your first run, the initial feelings of internal revolt, the nausea, the vomiting, and the dizziness will quickly pass. More than likely, you will be back to normal within half an hour, and you will probably have a residual sense of accomplishment that lasts for some time. You will also have plenty of reminders of that first running experience. Your ankles will probably be sore for several days, especially if you ran on asphalt or concrete. Your feet might be blistered or bruised. And your leg muscles will surely stiffen and ache. Fortunately, these are only minor acute problems, but there are more harmful long-term effects as well. Let me quickly review them for you in order to increase your awareness of running injuries and to further strengthen my case for walking.

In 1969, years before the current running mania, Dr. James Glick and Mr. Victor Katch collected some interesting data on the detrimental effects of jogging. The information was gathered from 120 participants between the ages of 19 and 65, over an 11-week period. Of the 120 individuals, 86 were novice joggers and 34 were experienced runners. For simplicity their injuries were classified according to the following list:

1. Muscle strains.
2. Joint sprains.
3. Tendon injuries.
4. Foot problems.
5. Fatigue fractures.
6. Back pain.
7. Rib injuries.
8. Miscellaneous problems.

In all, 241 injuries were noted! One hundred and eight of the 120 joggers had been injured. Forty-three percent of the injuries were muscle strains, 20 percent were joint sprains, and 18 percent were foot problems. Sixty-three percent of the muscle strains were located in the calf muscles and 21 percent in the hamstring muscles at the back of the thigh. Although only one jogger experienced painful swelling of the lower leg, (anterior chamber symdrome), 11 others were diagnosed as having "shin splints."

Blisters and arch strains accounted for most of the foot

problems, but heel pains described as "jogger's heel" and painful blood clots under the toenails were also noted.

Two fatigue fractures were diagnosed in one of the joggers but, being only minor cracks, they did not prevent the completion of the 11-week program. However, two less fortunate participants had to drop out because of severe muscular and joint problems.

As you can plainly see, there are a great many injuries, both insignificant and serious, that arise from running. Now that you know what you could face, let me tell you a little more about each ailment.

Joint disease:

Because running is really a series of continuous jumps, instead of the rather smooth glide of walking, it places tremendous strain on your joints. As you transfer your jolting weight from one foot to the other when you run, shock absorption must occur at the joint space, which results in compression and trauma to all joint surfaces. Consequently, the primary joints of running, the ankle, the knee, and the hip, are bound to incur some degree of injury. Other joints may also be affected.

Take the spine, for instance, which is actually composed of 32 small bones called vertebrae, and just as many joints. It sustains a tremendous pounding with every jogging step. You see, as your heel makes contact with a hard surface, the jolt is trasmitted up your leg, into your hip, and through your spine. This force is so tremendous, at times reaching 200 percent of body weight, that it eventually takes its toll somewhere along the line, either in the ankle, knee, hip, or spine—sometimes in all four areas plus the shoulders. The result: pain and discomfort that may last hours, days, or weeks. And, if running is a daily routine, the discomfort may be perpetual, leading to permanent physical damage.

In a short piece entitled "Harmful Effects of Jogging," Dr. Gene Hunder relates the story of a 47-year-old jogger who suffered irreparable joint damage during a three-year period of running. Based on the patient's complaint of progressive hip pain, and a series of X rays that were taken throughout the course of the examination, Dr. Hunder discovered degeneration and occlusion of the right hip joint—a serious disability. Writes Hunder, "The loss of about seventy-five percent of the joint space in eleven months was more rapid than would normally be expected and, in retrospect, it seems likely that the added jarring and shearing stress of rapid jogging may have accelerated the erosion of the (joint) cartilage. . . ."

Such injury is a good deal more serious than simple aches and pains. Once the cartilage of the hip, knee, or any other joint is damaged, it cannot heal itself adequately. Instead, scar tissue builds up, the joint becomes painful with movement, and repair must be made surgically. To me, this seems like a high price to pay for staying in shape.

Muscles:

Muscular soreness and stiffness, as I have mentioned, are also a consequence of running. But these are incidental problems that quickly pass, with or without medical treatment. Although they cause temporary discomfort, no residual effects are apparent.

Basically, the same is true of muscular strains. However, the damage here is slightly greater, and the healing time is longer, occasionally requiring several days to several weeks of inactivity.

Unfortunately, far more serious complications can also develop. They include partial muscular tears and total separations that require surgical intervention and literally months to heal.

At times, the healing of these wounds is incomplete, resulting in some degree of permanent loss and limitation of movement.

Because the muscles of acceleration, those in the calf and foot, are called upon to work hardest when you run, they are placed under the greatest stress and incur the most injuries. But physical damage also occurs in the hamstring muscles at the back of the thigh and the quadriceps across the front of the thigh.

Bones:

With jogging, the bones of your lower extremities take a beating too. Not only must they support the weight of your entire body, they must also accept the added stress of contracting muscles and the constant crash of the pavement beneath your feet. Consequently, all kinds of skeletal problems can arise.

From chondromalacia of the patella (softening of the kneecap) and stress fractures of the bones of the lower leg (the tibia and fibula), to impact breaks of the small bones of the foot and twisting fractures of the ankle itself, just about anything can happen. The medical journals are filled with such cases.

Shin Splints:

Although few runners realize what shin splints really are, they certainly know what they feel like—dull aching pain down the front of the lower leg. Here's how they occur.

Since the long arch of the foot becomes fatigued and weakened by constant pavement pounding, the foot tends to widen, and the foot bones separate. In turn, the ligaments of the ankle become stretched, and the muscles of the lower leg, resisting the stretch, are torn away from their bony attachments. When this happens, pain develops, as if you had damaged the shin itself.

Feet:

Your feet may revolt too!!

The friction of your running feet on the ground shows up as irritation at the toes and on the soles of your feet. As your heel rubs against the back of your shoe, the same thing happens. Eventually, your skin separates under this shearing pressure, and fluid fills in the gap to produce a raised, red, painful blister.

Painful inflammation of the Achilles tendon at the back of your heel might also occur. And, if your running is vigorous and sprintlike, a crippling tear of that tendon—yet another physical problem encountered by joggers—might develop instantaneously.

Less significant but still annoying foot problems associated with running include heel bruises, blackened toenails, sessamoiditis (inflammation of the small bones at the base of the big toe), and heel spurs—small, painful calcifications around the heel bone.

Brain:

Whenever you jog, your entire body is placed under tremendous stress. From the tip of your toes to the top of your head, everything is stimulated, especially your heart and lungs. Consequently, during each run, your pulse increases tremendously, your breathing becomes markedly labored, and your blood pressure temporarily goes up. This can cause serious trouble for the unconditioned, aging exerciser.

As I've discovered in the medical literature, older people occasionally succumb to strokes while running. As their blood pressure rises, they can overtax their hardened, atherosclerotic arteries and burst the vessels that are too weak to accommodate the added force. When this happens, blood escapes into the brain and destroys irreplacable neural tissue.

At other times, lack of oxygen to the brain produces the same effect, only in these cases it is the neural tissue and blood vessels that first die of oxygen starvation, leading to extensive intracranial bleeding that subsequently destroys even more of the brain substance. Either way, both conditions are disastrous and have been known to kill older joggers, particularly those with pre-existing high blood pressure.

Potential benefits aside, the risks of running are quite high. This fact cannot be ignored in the rush of media attention and public interest that has glorified the exercise and has enticed thousands upon thousands of unsuspecting and uneducated participants on to the streets and then into the hospital. While jogging has had its moment in the sun, these crucial facts have been lost in all the excitement. But they can be overlooked no longer.

Let's all exercise, but let's exercise safely, without the risk of serious injury. This can be done by choosing the most sensible form of aerobic activity, walking, and learning how to regulate its intensity. I am convinced, as I hope you are, that walking is the most reasonable approach and I urge you to make my program your new exercise guideline.

CHAPTER 19

Conclusion

I hope that after reading this book you now appreciate how great walking really is. In terms of total body conditioning, walking is far better than any of the isometric and isotonic exercises. In addition, it is as good for you as any aerobic exercise, even those that are much more strenuous, like running and jogging. This means that if you become serious about your walking, there is no reason why you can't be as fit as any swimmer, runner, or other avid exerciser. And, since walking is the safest of all exercises, you will not only get in shape, but also stay in shape, without the risk of serious injury, yet another key point.

The fabulous benefits of walking do not end here. Since walking is the only exercise that can be performed anytime, anywhere, it is easily incorporated into your daily schedule, making it totally practical. Perhaps this is walking's greatest advantage, for doctors and researchers now agree that we must exercise every day in order to obtain excellent fitness. Since walking is so easy to do, so beneficial and so safe, it is only logical for us to do it. Aren't you ready for a little more logic in today's physical fitness scene?

Far from being a new contortion for the unwary, walking is really our most natural exercise. Our entire body totally evolves around walking.

Of all the creatures, man is the one true walker. Why? Because millions of years ago, when primitive man first stood erect, he gave up running for walking. He became a rover and walked for days in search of food and lodging. Consequently, via the evolutionary process, we have been handed down an entire skeleton, bones and joints, and a majority of muscles that are literally made for walking. Not for running. Not for swimming. Not for jumping. Not for climbing. But for walking. It's man's natural exercise. It is the exercise for which our bodies have developed.

For this reason, walking has also been called man's most efficient exercise. With every step you take, you exercise over 50 percent of the muscles of your body, evenly, developing their natural shape in proportion to one another. You also limber up all of the joints of your body, gently, thus preserving their natural range of motion and normal function. In addition, you help to prevent or alleviate arthritis and the frozen joints that sometimes accompany that debilitating disease. Walking does it all, completely and efficiently, in the shortest time possible.

With these facts in mind, it's easy to understand how important walking really is in our lives. Walking can keep us in shape, naturally. Indeed, it's as natural to us as eating, sleeping, and even breathing.

Without a doubt, walking is the best exercise for the older

population because it isn't too strenuous, yet it provides good health and prevents illness. But don't think that all you 20-, 30-, and 40-year-olds are left out. You are the people who can benefit the most from the aerobic nature of walking. By establishing a sensible exercise program early in life, you will be far more likely to carry it on into your later years. You will not only be healthier now, but you will also be healthier at 60, 70, and 80. You can also expect to live a longer life.

Yes, walking does prolong life. Consider these two reports that appeared in *Executive Health,* an exciting new medical monthly.

"Meriden, March 24, 1961: Sidney J. Roby of Berlin, who was one hundred and four years old on Saint Valentine's Day, died today at Meriden Hospital. Mr. Roby was known for his love of walking. For many years he walked up to ten miles a day, but cut down to about an hour a day when he reached one hundred. . . ." (It's a shame he cut back!)

"Dr. Godfrey Lowell Cabot, founder and president of the Cabot Corporation, international manufacturers of chemicals, died in his sleep in his home here today. He was one hundred and one years old. Walking was to be his lifelong hobby. Until his doctors stopped him in his mid-nineties, Dr. Cabot had walked four miles a day. . . ." (Imagine how long he might have lived if he had continued to walk!)

Sure, these are just two isolated reports, but they do suggest an association between walking and long life. For more extensive evidence, consider the different peoples of the world who are noteworthy for their longevity—the Peruvian Valcabambas and the Soviet Georgians, you know, the yogurt people. Along with the East African Masai and the Pakistani Hunzas, these are cultures where great age is common. People live to be 120, 130, 140, and, yes, 150 years old. These are the cultures of the great centenarians.

In studying these people for clues to their long life, certain key factors appear over and over again. These are known as the great constants of longevity, and include good water and clean air, moderate eating and drinking, strong genes, stable emotions, hard work, sturdy health and regular physical activity. Interestingly, the physical activity most common to all the centenarians is *walking*. You see, the Georgians walk up to ten miles each day as they travel back and forth to work. Even the older people, those 120 and even 130 years old, walk extensively. Better yet are the Masai who cover up to 25 miles a day on their walks. They stay fit and trim and live long lives, confirming again the wondrous association between walking and longevity.

It's a happy surprise to discover that walking not only prolongs life, it also improves the quality of life. Among the centenarians, a zestful lifestyle is common. Most importantly, these people are virtually without anxiety and the other nervous disorders that plague modern societies like our own. Indeed, in America where the pace of life is hectic, stress and anxiety can be greatly reduced by walking your cares away. It has recently been reported that walking is probably as effective as Valium in relieving tension. It is nature's own tranquilizer.

But if a potentially longer and more relaxed lifestyle leaves you indifferent, remember that walking is one of the best aids to any diet. And in our youth-oriented society, everyone seems to be preoccupied with dieting these days. All of the aerobic exercises are great, but walking tends to reduce the legs and slim the buttocks the best. As for burning calories, walkers derive the same benefit as runners, consuming only 20 percent less calories mile for mile than the most enthusiastic jogger. Again, walking is far more efficient than you might have imagined.

We all know that walking aids digestion. Think back to those big Thanksgiving Day dinners and the natural desire to get up and walk around after eating. It was nature's way of telling you what was best for your body.

But here's something you might not know.

As you get older and your natural sugar metabolism slows down, there is a tendency for you to develop diabetes. Once diabetes begins, it usually becomes progressively worse and can lead to the destruction of your kidneys, heart, and brain, ultimately causing death. In large measure, diabetes can be prevented, retarded or actually reversed through walking, because your metabolic processes become more active and your body's sugar is utilized more easily by your exercising muscles. Many diabetics can throw their medication away after entering the walking program. Again, it is yet another example of the fabulous aerobic results.

Well, there you have it. I rest my case. Obviously, I'm convinced that walking is the best way to prevent many diseases and to live a long and healthy life. I hope you agree. Truly, it is a medical miracle, and we should all come to our senses about it. Review the evidence for yourself.

1. Walking is the one exercise we can do anytime, anywhere.
2. Walking is the safest form of exercise we can get.
3. Walking is the most natural exercise for human beings.
4. Walking is the most efficient way to exercise.
5. Walking is the only exercise that we can perform at any age.
6. Walking reduces stress and promotes relaxation.
7. Walking strengthens our bones and gently massages our joints, thus preventing many of the skeletal problems we suffer.
8. Walking burns calories and aids weight reduction.
9. Walking increases our heart and lung capacities.
10. Walking expands our circulatory system.

11. Walking lowers the blood pressure and the resting pulse.
12. Walking prevents or reverses diabetes.
13. Walking aids digestion.
14. Walking retards the aging process.
15. Walking is the very best way to prevent a host of additional diseases and generally preserve good health.
16. Walking is a great form of transportation.

Please heed the warnings and adhere to the logic. Walk for your life. It will make us all happier.